From
DEBT
to
DESTINY

Creating Financial Freedom
from the Inside Out

GENEIN M. LETFORD, MEd

D0971452

From Debt to Destiny

Creating Financial Freedom from the Inside Out

Copyright © 2019 Genein M. Letford, MEd

ISBN: 978-1-080232-60-4

This book is dedicated to my grandmothers:

Della Marie Cantrell,
who gave her time to help church folk with their finances, and

Emily Victoria Jefferson,
who always reminded me, "Don't take no wooden nickels!"

*You both gave me the courage to be **bold** and share my story while having the **compassion** to love and teach others. I stand on your shoulders and thank God I had the privilege to come through your lineage. I love and miss you both.*

Partial proceeds of this book will support financial and creative arts classroom projects on Donorschoose.org. Visit Donorschoose.org to support a classroom today!

Praise for *Debt to Destiny*

"The timing of this book is perfect! Creative thinking when it comes to our finances ensures a life of freedom and direction. Genein is gifted at making complicated ideas easy to understand and she does a great job of reminding us that our lives and our money each have a purpose, one that is tied to our destiny!"

—Yvette Nicole Brown, actress/host/education advocate

"Genein's disciplined effort to eliminate the crushing debt from her life has opened doors of opportunity for others. Genein proudly shares her secrets so you too have the ability to pursue your dreams."

—Gina Hagen, former CFO, Milani Cosmetics and OPI Nails

"The greatest thing about the content Genein imparts to her readers is the results it has produced; Individuals getting out of debt, financial freedom in people oppressed by circumstances, others getting control of their life again. She wonderfully illustrates how people's creative gifts do not have to be sacrificed but are actually utilized in the process of financial breakthrough."

—Trey Fernald, artistic director & founder of
Eastern Sky Theatre Company

"Financial literacy is not only life changing but essential in becoming successful in life. When I was 16 my kidneys failed while my parents were losing their jobs during the 2008 recession. Having no financial plan and no money, our lives changed forever, and my parents filed for bankruptcy. Life events happen and applying the strategies from this book will position you to overcome them. Genein shares powerful lessons, experiences, and triumphs throughout her book that not only inspire you but empowers you to be creative and use that creativity to produce results. Use these lessons to build your financial foundation so you have the resources to create the life you want!"

—Christian Carreon, founder of All One Wealth Investment Firm

"As an economist turned entrepreneur, I've learned that creativity and success go hand in hand because you constantly have to make the most out of the resources available to you. Genein challenges you to see opportunity where others see challenges and forces you to think outside of the box. She truly inspires your creativity to spark innovation."

—Samah, founder of Festoun Fashion Social Enterprise

"Finance and creative literacy plays a vital role in creating a better future for all. It helps prevent the poor from being exploited, provides hope for a better life, and transforms potential into opportunity. Genein's lessons really guides you through this process of creating a solid financial foundation."

—Scott Glasgow, founder of FinMango

"Genein teaches from a place of wisdom, not just regurgitating something she saw in a book. With applying the teaching and concepts in Debt to Destiny, my wife and I have flipped our house right side up. The mindset this book teaches on and the use of your own creativity for your financial success can really set you free. Start small and watch the snowball grow into an avalanche of greatness in your own life."

—Lee Hughes, Columbia College Hollywood
admissions advisor, entrepreneur, investor

FOREWORD

Debt is an unruly, slave driver that has deprived people from their destiny way too long. Trust me, I know how difficult it is to spread your wings and dream upward–high in the clouds of possibilities–when you are earthbound by an all-consuming weight of debt. The good news is, you do not need to miss out on a financially secure future and the door to destiny that is waiting for you. There is hope! And I believe you'll find that in the pages of this book.

I remember the day that Genein hosted a financial workshop at our venue. I was there simply to set up before the students arrived because I had another commitment that day. When it came time for me to exit, I noticed Genein had planted a blank sheet of paper on each desk. Naturally I assumed she was providing extra note-taking material for her students, only to find out it was a tactical object lesson. One that would awaken me from living in a cycle of financial deficiency. The piece of paper represented the plan that most people have when it pertains to managing their financial future…and that is why it was blank.

The truth is, none of us ever planned on living in a constant state of "owing" during our adult life. But the problem is, we also did not plan to not be in debt. When we are void of any sort of plan for our finances, we become vulnerable to a system that is designed to sell us a lifestyle that comes with a cost. Usually the cost of our financial freedom.

My story is a very common story. I worked hard and succeeded in my profession, yet I had become another statistic. A man in his early forties, without any lucrative investments or sufficient retirement plan, a loaded credit card bill, and a tiny savings account. That all changed once Genein widely opened my eyes and personally began to guide me to do what I seemed to not be able to accomplish in my lifetime. Within a year, I reduced my credit card balance to zero, I began a retirement fund, and I was able to secure money in my savings account. This was a huge change for me. I was finally heading in the right direction once I found what was missing. I just needed a Genein Letford; an instrumental, empowering voice, filled with truth, wisdom, and a heart to help the world come to the knowledge of financial literacy and their right to be free from debt.

What I love about *From Debt to Destiny* is that it is not just a book with a step-by-step outline to conquer the financial mountain. The brilliance behind the work of Genein Letford is the foundation that is passed on to us. Getting out of debt is one thing, but it is more valuable thing to build core values that recreate our relationship with money, use our creativity to improve our wealth and renew the structure of our perception when it comes to life in its fullness.

Jump on in and learn from a woman who has lived on both sides of the coin, who has gone from a position of overwhelming debt that seemed hopeless to a life filled with hope, promise, and possibilities. I believe this book is what you have been looking for. It will dramatically make all the right adjustments in your life. I encourage you to get started on your journey to freedom today. Your destiny is waiting for you.

Tymme Reitz
Pastor, Speaker, Author of
In the Waiting and *Living Souled Out*

CONTENTS

INTRODUCTION

Hey there. It's so good to be with you right now! Come, have a seat next to me. I just want to chat with you about this thing called money. This book is a heart-to-heart talk on the real issue of why most of our finances are a mess. If your money is a mess, I know what you're going through. I've been there.

As I'm writing this book, I'm an elementary school teacher, living on a teacher's salary. Throughout my struggles, and eventually triumphs, I became aware of the key strategies and insights on fixing my finances but also became aware of my relationship with money. Yep, that's right. I am in a relationship with money. So are you. I want to make sure it's not taking advantage of you. I'm here to walk through my experience and help you get through yours.

You might have heard some of these ideas, and some might be new, but it's all part of what helped me begin the journey to become debt free, learning how to build wealth and finally have a healthy relationship with money.

I'm an academic, but this isn't an academic book. I've written a thesis, and this is nothing like it. You won't find information on bull and bear markets, thick data on the implications of the economical shifts, or the decreasing countervailing power of the middle class. Nope. Not here.

This is just me, being real with you. Like we're having a conversation, sittin' on the front porch with a glass of homemade lemonade and my grandmother's peach cobbler.

You will find just how we got into this mess and how we can get out. You will see that this process is more than numbers and spreadsheets. It's more than just skipping that latte or cutting that coupon.

It's a game.

That's right.

You're in a game, and you didn't even know it. This whole thing is a game and most of us who are playing don't even know the rules.

I titled this book *Creating Financial Freedom from the Inside Out* because it's the inner areas that need to be addressed before the outer areas can really see a sustained result. The *outer areas* are the external numbers—the budgets, the debt, the graphs. The *inner areas* are the unseen components, which includes your mindset, the subconscious effect of consumerism, and your identity. It's like playing a game of basketball. You need to be mindful of the offense and the defense. The same is true with our money.

When people think about getting their finances in order, they only think about spending less and saving more. They might look at their numbers. They might not. But what they don't realize is all the inner-game factors that are at play and all the outer-game factors are playing them. We're being played like a cracked violin with three strings—out of tune and not performing at our full potential. It's time to change that tired song. It's time to get some new melodies. Throughout this book, we'll look at these game factors, play by play, and we'll identify them.

We're getting back in the driver's seat.

I remember asking God, "God, I'm a music teacher. I have a degree in psychology and a master's degree in education. Why am I so passionate about finances and so consumed with helping people get a handle on their money?"

This book was his answer. I felt God say, "Genein, it's more about the mind than the money. It's more about identity than income. This isn't just debt payments, this is people's destinies at stake. You know how to educate people, help them to increase their creativity in order to create financial breakthroughs. You understand the psychology behind it all. You're the one."

So here I am. Like Nero from the *Matrix*. Ready to reveal the truth.

Americans are looking around, asking questions. "How are my wages stagnate but food, gas, and rent prices keep rising? Why are companies laying off so many people, but they are showing records profits? I got my degree, but I'm buried in debt and stuck working at Starbucks! How did I get $5,000 on this credit card? I don't even remember what I bought!"

Our universal question is, "How did I get here?"

I've been there, as you're about to see. I have felt your pain and cried your cry. This book is the response to the financial suicide I see so many of my peers and young students blindly headed toward. This is my attempt to throw down a rope to them and help them find their way out.

So, lace up your shoes. Stretch those muscles. Get ready, because the ball is heading your way.

It's now in your court.

Get ready for the game of your life.

Section One
MAKE A DECISION

Chapter One

(Inner Game)
DECIDE TO RIDE

There she was, crying in my classroom. As she glanced around at the walls, looking at nothing in particular, she lamented, "I'm working so much. I just don't know where it all goes. Why am I still broke?"

Brenda, who I've known since she was in the third grade as her music teacher, was seeing a glimpse of where her life was headed. And she didn't like it one bit. At sixteen, with two part-time jobs and carrying a full load in high school, she was just beginning her financial journey and knew she was already headed in the wrong direction.

"I just don't want to end up like so many people I see around me. I don't want to struggle all my life," she shared between the gentle sobbing.

I knew then that this meeting was not a random encounter but a divine appointment.

"It seems like this meeting was meant to be," I replied softly. "Are you ready to make a decision?"

Decide to Ride

"It is in your moments of decision
that your destiny is shaped."

—TONY ROBBINS

Brussel sprouts—kale—arugula, do these foods make your mouth water? Me neither. Isn't it odd that so many things that are good for us aren't that appealing (like Brussel sprouts and zucchini)? I don't know about you, but I don't jump out of bed in the morning with excitement to add kale to my smoothie. Zero calories and zero taste.

On the flip side, there are quite a few items that might cause you to sing their praises whenever they're in your sight. Krispy Kreme donuts, potato chips (you really can't eat just one!), and deep-fried chicken. Need I go on?

But really? Who are we kidding? We know those aren't the best choices for us, but who cares about that as we send them to their final resting place on our tongues? They taste like mini samples of heaven!

These combinations are not fair. Junk food that tastes wonderful but will poison your body and eventually kill you. Healthy food that is not too titillating on the tongue but is needed for us to be alert and alive.

If I had my way, sugar cookies and caramel-covered ice cream would be included in every regimen for weight loss and a healthy lifestyle. But they're not. Eating right has to be an intentional choice, or we will unconsciously resort to the cultural default—junk food and sugary drinks.

This is reality—it's la la land. And in the world of la la land, people are broke, terribly unhealthy, and living their lives without purpose. Now is the time when we demand better from ourselves and our nation.

Society doesn't demand we eat sensibly. We have to demand it of ourselves. Glasses of water don't call out our names. We have to choose to drink enough water. Culture doesn't force us to learn about money and consume with wisdom and restraint. We have to be intentional to learn and implement those lessons ourselves.

This is on us.

It's easy to choose options that don't really cost us anything—or rather we let culture make these selections for us. When fast food joints pop up on every corner, it takes an extra effort to seek out healthy food choices and do the research on the best options for our families.

When advertisements to spend bombard us on billboards, television, and even in the middle of your Pandora playlist, it takes extra time to track expenses, haggle for the best deal, and discuss the reasons we won't buy a $800 drone for our eight-year-old son for Christmas, even though all his friends have one.

Bottom line, if we want things to be different, we need to be different. We need to make a decision. Yea, I said the "D" word.

Decision.

There it is again.

Indecision is the thief of opportunity. Indecision is costly. Whether you are being crushed under $90,000 worth of debt with charged-off accounts and a dismal credit score of 580, or you're a college kid freakin' out with a $400 balance on a credit card, making a decision is, and will always be, the first step.

Do you want to keep living like this? Do you want to keep treading water not really moving anywhere financially—or worse yet—drowning?

Decision. Decision. Decision.

Make a decision!

You don't have to be so afraid of that word—because guess what? You just did it. You already made one decision that's moving you in the right direction. You bought this book. You opened it! You're actually reading it!

Smile! Here's looking at you kid!

Rock Your Bottom

*"Rock bottom became the solid foundation on which
I rebuilt my life."*

—J.K. ROWLING

Every person has their rock bottom. For me, it was sitting on that living room floor with a Bank of America credit card bill in my hand, weeping uncontrollably. You'd have thought I was a toddler who just had her toy ripped from her hands.

This breaking point varies from person to person. For some, it could be as tragic as losing a house or not being able to get the basic necessities of life. For others, it could occur when the service is interrupted on their cell phone (oh, I've been there before) or their card is declined, yet again, in an endless line at Target. Whatever that point is for you, it is usually the point where you realize there is nowhere else to go but up. You're thinking, "I'm done living like this. I can no longer accept this as the norm of my life."

Or better yet—"Ain't nobody got time for this!"

Whatever vernacular you choose to use, to go up, you must make a clear decision to do so. You can let that rock bottom be the dismal end or you can "rock your bottom" and let it be your launching pad. I chose the latter. It made all the difference in my life. I hope you will choose to go up too.

Normally, quite a few our decisions are made for us, especially earlier in life. The decision of where to attend primary school and the decision of our faith—or absence thereof—are usually initiated by our parents. Starting in adolescence, the decisions to dress a certain way or do a certain activity that might have awful consequences are usually brought on by our peers. Me sporting Cross Colours clothing, high bangs, and putting lipstick on my cheeks in junior high school was certainly not a choice I came to on my own! It was a choice I was encouraged to make by those I surrounded myself with.

We are humans, and humans are highly influenced by social contact. Even though we think we are in control of our lives, many of our decisions are being made subconsciously for us through culture. We'll dive deeper into this concept in section four.

But understand that once you make the firm decision to win at this game of personal finance, you will be going against the cultural grain in many areas of your life. You'll be swimming against the stream and running against the pack. This is not a task for the weak, and you are not weak. I'm serious. You are not weak. Still, your discipline muscles have to be strengthened to climb out of this. This does not happen by accident. This happens by setting a standard and then raising it and knowing why you're ready to fight this fight.

Know Your Why

There have been stories of the most amazing feats done by physically average people. For instance, a 135-pound woman actually lifted a car off her screaming child. How did she do it? She had a fairly good reason— the life of her child—and her body went into hyper mode and found hidden strength. It's amazing what we can do when we have clearly laid out our reasons.

Reasons bring results. Strong reasons bring strong results.

Have you stopped to ask yourself these questions?

+ What are my reasons?
+ Why do I want to get out of debt?
+ Why do I want to make more money?
+ Why do I need to get control of my finances?
+ Why?

Instead of focusing on your debt, or the late charges, or the pile of bills, switch your focus to the image of you having more than enough. Entertain the image of your children or family enjoying life without the stresses of scraping together the rent or yelling at the electric company to turn your lights back on. Picture yourself donating to the nearby homeless center or buying books for your local classroom and reading the students' thank-you letters, because you made their day. Think about those end results to the decision you're making today.

Close your eyes and picture a life with no financial stress.

Now, breathe in and say, "I'm ready to decide on a better choice."

Stop Fooling Yourself

> "The first principle is that you must not fool
> yourself—and you are the easiest person to fool."
> —RICHARD P. FEYNMAN

"Don't put this on your mother," he said, looking at me. "This is your fault."

Allen Sharp had the most piercing blue eyes that seemed to strike directly into my soul. Sitting with my first professional mentor, I was surprised and honored he agreed to meet with me after years of not seeing him. A powerful force in the real estate development sector, he managed multimillion-dollar construction projects and was one of the toughest negotiators this side of the Mississippi River. This is one man whose good side I wanted to stay on.

Blinking, I chose my words carefully. "What do you mean?"

"Well, you can claim that you're not financially fit because your mom didn't show you, or the schools didn't teach you. But, in the end, this is your fault."

"How so?" I retorted, with my feelings a little hurt. "How am I supposed to know these things if no one taught me?"

"How long have you been reading? How long have you known where the library is?"

I started to see where he was going. I averted my gaze.

In every conversation we have had, Allen has always been blunt with me. Even though he served up the truth with a side of sting, I knew he cared. Message received. He was telling me that the alphabet in itself is an abolitionist.

"Genein, you've written a long list as to why you're not where you want to be financially. Continue to add whatever you want on there—the economy, low teacher salaries, your race, your gender, the color of your car—whatever! It doesn't matter!"

I kept listening.

"Because until your name is on that list, nothing will change." He stopped to offer a warm smile, softening the harsh blow as only he could. "So, stop fooling yourself, take responsibility. It's only then you can start making things happen!"

He knew what I have now come to know. It's easy to shift the blame to others for the outcome of our adult lives. So easy. I tried to pass the "blame game" ball, but he blocked me at every pivot. The first sign of maturity is being someone who can take responsibility for their actions and their life.

Believe me, I know some of us have really good excuses as to why we are where we are. No matter how the past played out—if you experienced a tumultuous childhood, if you had relationship trouble or your supervisor was straight up trippin'—today is a new day. You now have the strength to take responsibility for what happens from here on out. This is your story. The ball is in your hand. It's time to play, and it's time to play to win.

Taking responsibility for where I was in life—thirty, brilliant, and broke—was not easy, but it was the catalyst that moved me in the right direction. I had been working since I was fifteen years old (go Kmart!) and still had a negative net worth. I took responsibility for that track record, extracted the lessons, made a decision, and started moving forward, one step at a time. The next step was knowing which direction to move toward. This is where the goals come in.

Chapter Two

(Inner Game)
GET TO THOSE GOALS

Where's the Basket?

"Setting goals is the first step in turning the invisible into the visible."

—TONY ROBBINS

Imagine a soccer or football game without the goalposts. Hysterical! All you have is hyped-up athletes running all over the place with no particular focus. Wasted time and wasted energy. That was the game of finance I was once in. My chaotic life of kicking the ball in any direction, praying it got into the goal that didn't even exist, was how I lived with my money. Is that the game you're in? Time to play a new game. After you've made a definite decision, it is imperative to learn how to set effective goals.

Setting goals isn't "nice to do when I have time" or "I'll see when I can get to it." It's a critical move for any type of success in any area of growth—physical, spiritual, professional, etc. You have to have a direction to move in and something to shoot for. You can do this well by employing SMART goals.

SMART goals are specific, measurable, achievable, relevant, and timebound. Getting out of the land of ambiguity and coming into clarity will greatly increase your success rate.

- Specific (simple, sensible, significant)
- Measurable (meaningful, motivating)
- Achievable (agreed, attainable)
- Relevant (reasonable, realistic, results-based)
- Timebound (time based, time limited, time sensitive)

Some authors have expanded the SMART concept to include the important process of reviewing and feedback; SMARTER goals include Evaluate and Review. As an educator, I encourage people to take a step back to reflect on why or why not their goal was reached. There's power in efficient reflection.

SMARTER Goal

How is it Specific? Are you clear in what you are achieving?	
How is it Measurable? When do you know you have reached it?	
How is it Achievable? Have you listed the baby steps to reach it?	
How is it Relevant? Is this goal connected to your financial overall goal?	

How is it Timebound? How long will it take? Did you set an endpoint when you want to reach the goal?	
Evaluate Consider the components that made the goal successful or unsuccessful.	
Review Review the entire process. Keep what worked and adjust what did not work. Add in accountability partners if need be. Set new goals.	

Can you evaluate and review this goal? Once again, goals, for most people, are like the weather; everybody talks about it, but no one does anything about it. But unlike the weather, setting goals is something we can actually implement to help us move in the right direction. There are people counting on us to become financially fit, and one of those people is you.

> *"We must all suffer from one of two pains: the pain of discipline or the pain of regret.*
>
> *The difference is discipline weighs ounces while regret weighs tons."*
>
> —Jim Rohn

Chapter Three

(Inner Game)
THE YOU INSIDE
OF YOU

*"You cannot escape the responsibility of tomorrow
by evading it today."*

—ABRAHAM LINCOLN

Seventy-Nine-Year-Old Genein: Stop Pissing Her Off

People watching is fun, especially at Venice Beach, California. There are some—how do I say this nicely—*interesting* characters walking along that boardwalk. And I mean interesting [wink-wink]. Some people gaze at the clouds drifting by and imagine what they could be. I'd rather people watch and wonder who they chose to be.

Every now and then I will gaze at an elderly person, walking much slower than the young, bright-eyed kids whizzing past. I see a woman in her seventies and think, *Wow, she was once my age. She was even a third-grade student in somebody's class.* But here she is, with spotted hands and a wrinkled face, softened with a warm smile. She's totally at ease with letting the caterpillars beat her to the grass.

Those observations grounded me. I am yet again reminded that, God willing, I will one day be her age, moving a little slower than I do now, abhorring the dark spots adorning my arms and hands. (I just got three new spots last month—ugh!) I'll be old. It was then I realized that twenty-something Genein—who spent all her paycheck on random stuff, put everything on credit cards, and was paying tons of unneeded interest—was pissing off elderly Genein.

Greatly.

Left: Genein, thirty-seven years old. Right: Genein, seventy-nine years old. (I still look good!)

This resonated with me so much, I even printed a photo of her. The apps AgingBooth or Oldify will take my current face and make it look old. Yep, elderly Genein didn't look too happy with my previous choices. It was as if I could hear her speaking to me.

"Genein, being old isn't bad. You're wiser, and you've seen things. You understand what's really important in life. But let me tell you, being old and broke, those are two words you don't want to combine. Get your act together, girl!"

Elderly Genein whooped my butt.

Can you hear the older version of yourself reprimanding you right now?

"Seriously, sonny? Do you really need to sign up for a new car lease every three years? You're putting $500 into that car that you'll never own but nothing into an account for me? Now we're stuck living in poverty, on Medicaid, and eating cat food. Forget the car! Forget the freakin' car!"

Don't piss the elderly you off. S/he needs you to live life and enjoy yourself but also be diligent and wise with your financial choices. Today's decisions manifest tomorrow's results. By making a clear decision today and setting goals, you'll be setting the old you up in a better situation.

Go to your app store and search for AgingBooth (which is free) or Oldify (which is ninety-nine cents as of 2019). Download the app and take a picture of the elderly you. Print it out and paste it here. Talk to her or him, to you. Write a letter about the reasons why this decision needs to happen now. Don't forget to share your goals with the old you.

The Current You	The Old You

Letter from Current You to Old You

As you keep reading, we'll continue to set clear goals and create the plan of execution. You can even meet with your elderly self to review these goals! You can do this. I know you can. You're on the right team. Now, let's get to the numbers.

Call to Action

I, _____, have made the decision to live a financially responsible life. I will do the work to control my finances, set goals, and be aware of the progress or struggles that I experience.

Sign and Date

Section One Summary

1. Make a decision to take responsibility for your financial situation.
2. Make a clear decision to become financially literate.
3. Set clearly defined goals that are measurable and timebound.
4. Be mindful of the "old you" on the inside that is counting on you to be financially wise.

Section Two
DANCING WITH THE NUMBERS

Chapter Four

(Outer Game)
THE MONSTER
IN THE CLOSET

*"You can't conquer what you don't confront, and
you can't confront what you don't identify."*

—PAULA WHITE

With its pictures of a jazz artist on every wall, my twin sister's apartment had a musical feel. Music has a large place in her life. On many occasions, I find myself scanning her extensive CD collection of greats stacked in the corner. Ray Charles, Charlie Parker, and Billie Holiday, to name a few. This time another stack caught my eye.

"What's in these envelopes?" I asked, pointing at the ominous pile of envelopes that were on the verge of toppling over.

"Those?" she responded, with a look of exasperation. "Girl, those are my student loans." Rolling her eyes, she added, "And some are in default. I just don't know where to start—so I just leave them over there. Out of sight, out of mind."

This is called the ostrich syndrome, when people stick their heads in the sand to avoid something uncomfortable. Sadly, she's not alone.

With the rising cost of college tuition, many Generation X and Millennial kids got caught in the student loan tidal wave. Some of us didn't just get caught, we got obliterated in the storm. In fact, the whole alphabet soup of X, Y, and Z generations are drowning in this current crisis. Student loan debt is the second largest debt in America, behind mortgage debt, and has surpassed $1.56 trillion as of 2019.[1] One in four Americans has student loan debt, with the average student graduating with over $37,000 of debt.[2] Genae isn't alone in the land of default. In fact, she has plenty of company. With a national default rate of 11.5 percent,[3] there are thousands of ostriches all around her, also sticking their heads in the sand.

Power Position

Hiding from the problem isn't going to make it go away. Yes, sometimes it can seem overwhelming and downright daunting. I know it did for me. Those feelings were surrounding me when I pressed "enter" on the calculator and totaled my debt for the first time. My husband and I owed $92,543! You know the emoji with the wide eyes? That was me. Disbelief coupled with fear.

But once you gather the courage to face the numbers head on, you realize they are only numbers. It's not someone with a gun to your head. There's no grizzly bear chasing you up a tree. It's not someone pushing you out of a plane without a parachute.

---

[1] "A Look at the Shocking Student Loan Debt Statistics for 2019." February 4, 2019. See https://studentloanhero.com/student-loan-debt-statistics/.

[2] Abigail Hess. "Here's How Much the Average Student Loan Borrower Owes When They Graduate." February 15, 2018. See https://www.cnbc.com/2018/02/15/heres-how-much-the-average-student-loan-borrower-owes-when-they-graduate.html

[3] "A Look at the Shocking Student Loan Debt Statistics for 2019."

They are just numbers.

These numbers include your net worth, total debt, expenses, and cash flow. Knowing your numbers, you can start to devise a plan; you can begin to negotiate better conditions. You will have a true starting point when you set your goals.

But having your head in the sand, humming to your own "I can't see it, so it doesn't exist" song will not only delay progress, but it will leave you in an even worse position as time progresses.

When it comes to student loans—they ain't no joke.

Due to legislation, they are the worst consumer-protected type of debt out there. They cannot be written off, even in dire situations (only in rare exceptions), the government can garnish your wages, your disability payments, and even your Social Security checks if you remain in default and don't work out a payment plan. This gives the old you yet another reason to scream your head off!

My Bank of America credit card bill had my husband and me by the neck. It was strangling us, and if there was a bill to hide from, this was it. The monthly payment was $250 with $161 going to interest. It was like someone punched me in the stomach.

Nevertheless, we made a decision and set our goal to get rid of the debt. I scraped up the courage to call the credit card company and get some options about slaying this dragon. Many companies would rather work with you than have you stop paying them, which results in the account being charged-off (or sent to a collections agency). So, once we started communicating with the Bank of America supervisors, they decided to work with us. I give more details about how this played out in section nine.

Many of your bills and debts right now might show themselves as monsters in the closet. You might be hearing their loud roars in your mind or turning your head at the clawing sounds of their sharp nails on the door. When you think about them, you're imagining their gigantic, furry claws getting ready to rip apart your sanity and peace. But just think of Sully from *Monsters, Inc.*—or better yet, the spherical one-eyed Mike Wazowski and his goofy grin. They're not truly what they seem when you turn on the light, open your eyes, and see the true picture.

Throughout the rest of this section, we're going to learn how to navigate through these numbers and different types of debt to get a clear picture of what you might be up against. No more monsters. No more aliens. They are just numbers ready for competition.

> *"I am an old man and have known a great many*
> *troubles, but most of them never happened."*
>
> —MARK TWAIN

Chapter Five

(Outer Game)
Nothing but
Net . . . Worth

Starting Blocks

Ready—set—go!

"Runners to your mark," the announcer calmly called in a baritone voice. Eight runners with legs rivaling powerful horses walked confidently to their starting blocks. Sitting in the stands, I turned to my mother, who was eating popcorn.

"Mom, why is that guy way in front of the others?" I asked her while the runners strutted to their starting places for the 200-meter race. The wind was calm, and the sky was clear. Perfect weather to break a record. This was my first professional track meet, and the excitement was palpable.

"That's called a stagger," she responded, throwing another kernel in her mouth.

I immediately looked confused. "Stagger?"

"Yep. See, it looks like that runner in the outside lane is ahead," she grabbed another handful of popcorn, "but the farther you are from the inside of the track, the farther it is from the finish line," she explained. I turned my gaze to the lanes on the field. The runners were bouncing up and down behind the blocks.

"So, to make it fair, they move the starting points in the outside lanes farther up," she added.

"How do you know who's really winning?" I asked, trying to understand the concept.

"We have to wait until they hit the final straightaway, right there," she pointed at the last 100 meters before the finish line. "That's when you really have the best idea of who's really ahead versus who just *looks* like they're ahead."

"Set," the announcer yelled in a stern, clear voice. A silence blanketed the audience. I held my breath, still feeling sorry for the runner in lane one, who seemed to be behind everyone else.

"Go!" and the runners were off.

True North: A Staggering Net Worth

With the advent of credit, it's so easy to *look* like we're financially ahead in life. Many people use their purchases to give the illusion that they are doing well. It looks that way until they hit that last straightaway mark in their financial race; until that stagger is no longer apparent and the truth is revealed. That financial mark, that true north, is called your net worth.

There's a funny commercial that I show my clients and students in my financial creative seminars.[4] It's shows a man, Stanley Johnson, telling viewers about his beautiful four-bedroom house, his new car, his golf club membership, and happily cutting the grass on his personal lawn mower. He's sharing all these beautiful possessions he owns. We think he is the epitome of the American dream.

Or so it would seem.

---

[4]   "I'm in Debt Up to My Eyeballs. Lending Tree. See https://www.youtube.com/watch?v=PV_YAeXOSiw.

Amusingly, he smiles and looks at the camera.

"How do I do it?" he asks. "I'm in debt up to my eyeballs! I can barely pay my finance charges."

"Somebody help me!" he implores, before the company logo pops up.

I laugh every time I watch it. But honestly, it's not that funny.

Stanley represents a majority of American consumers. It looks like he's ahead in this race, running like sprinters Usain Bolt or Michael Johnson, with gold shoes and everything! But when the gun goes off and he rounds that corner, his debts are acting like ankle weights, weighing him down at every turn.

It almost looks like he's running backward. He's focused more on consuming goods to portray a certain lifestyle rather than building his net worth and living a purposeful life. Other people might be in this position because of certain economic situations, like low wages and rising living expenses.

Whatever the precursor to your financial strain, knowing your net worth is vital. What is net worth and why is it important? Let's find out.

Net Worth: A Vital Calculation

"Genein? Genein Letford?" I looked up as the nurse called my name. This was my first time at this doctor's office. I headed through the door.

"Hi, Doctor, I don't feel too well. My chest hurts badly. I'm dizzy. My heart feels like it's about to jump out of my body." I lifted my finger to his eye level. "Oh, and I have this paper cut on my finger too that stings like nobody's business."

"All right. I hear you. Well, first let's look at that paper cut and get that resolved," replied the physician, rifling through his drawer for a bandage.

If this ever happens to you at the doctor's office, run. Run far and run fast. Go find another physician. Why? Because you will more than likely die under this physician's care.

Do you know the first order of business when you visit the doctor?

The nurse checks your vitals. Not your fingers, not your stubbed toe, but your vitals. This includes your blood pressure, your heartbeat, your respirations, and your weight.

Though this seems like a mundane routine procedure, it is a critical move and will save your life. What difference does it make if you have a paper cut but your blood pressure is at the dangerous level of 160/120? Why give attention to a rash when your heartbeat is irregular and spastic?

A physician who knows what they are doing will always check to make sure your vitals are stabilized before they address other, less urgent concerns. The vitals give life to the organism in which they reside. Your vitals give information and data so the doctor can develop a course of action and determine what to attend to first.

This is the first step in the journey to physical fitness and vitality. For your finances, it is no different. What are your vitals in the world of financial health? Your net worth and your cash-flow numbers are your financial vitals.

Attend to these first.

Who cares what type of car you drive or if you prefer the Louis Vuitton purse over a Coach bag if you are bleeding out financially and can't pay your rent?

What does it matter if you own forty pairs of Air Jordans or if the bottom soles on your 5-inch heels are red, black, orange, or yellow, if the utility companies are about to turn off your lights, water, and heat?

So many of us are walking around, bleeding out uncontrollably, with dollar bills gushing out of our sides. We are all the while unaware of the future opportunities, possibilities, and life experiences leaving us—all because we haven't checked our vitals.

From this day forward, that will no longer be you. You'll now learn how to check your financial vitals, when to update them, and how to respond to the data you get from them.

Net Worth: A Simple Calculation

Say cheese! You're about to take a picture of your finances. Your net worth is a financial snapshot of your overall financial standing. It tells you how healthy, or unhealthy, your financial situation truly is.

Calculating net worth is simple. If you have a second-grade education, you can do this. You don't even need fancy data sheets. A blank piece of paper with a nice bold line down the middle will do.

First, take all your assets and write them on one side of a paper. An asset (for this exercise) is anything that you own that has value. This is your house, car, jewelry, cash in your wallet, money in a retirement account, and, yes, even that home gym that's been collecting dust for the past year.

When calculating the value of your furniture, determine what it would sell for if you listed it at a garage sale. Be realistic. The worst type of deception is self-deception.

Now, if any of these items has a debt against it, subtract that amount from its estimated value. The number you get is the true asset value of the item. For instance, if you bought a car that is worth $20,000 but you still owe $15,000 for that car, the financial amount you can claim toward your net worth is $5,000.

Once you are done adding up the value of everything you own (minus the debt), total the number and write it on the left side.

On the right side of the paper, write down everything you owe and *everyone* you owe.

This includes, but is not limited to, your mortgage, car loans, credit cards, school loans, personal loans, and the fifty dollars Jimmy let you "hold" until your next payday. Write down everything. This is not the time to fool ourselves nor is it the time to "soften" numbers because we're afraid of what the total will be. Remember that monster in the closet? It sounds scary, but once you really see it, it won't be that bad. I promise.

Our Eye-Opening Net Worth

After six months of marriage and deep in debt, my husband Shayne and I decided to get our financial situation together. And where did we start? With our vitals, of course, our net worth. Needless to say, the number was a bit shocking. I figured I'd been working since I was fifteen years old and I'd had my professional job as an educator for five years, so it can't be that bad, right?

Wrong.

It was -$50,000. Let me say it again, "negative fifty thousand dollars!"

Now that's a sobering number that will force anyone to wake up.

I kept thinking, *Wow, I've been a teacher for five years. My gross salary is about $46,000 a year. That's a total of $230,000 that has gone through me, and I have nothing—absolutely nothing—to show for it!"*

I had less than nothing. I had a negative net worth of -$50,000.

Though I was astonished—and a bit embarrassed—I was grateful to see that number. I was grateful because, like being on the floor crying over that Bank of America bill, it galvanized me even more to make a definitive decision to change my situation. It also gave me a clear metric of my starting point and how to track my progress and set goals. Knowing your net worth isn't just for millionaires or corporations; it's for everyone who wants to build a financial foundation and move their financial needle.

2009 Letford Family Net Worth

Item	Value	Debt	Equity
SL Toyota Celica	$15,000	-$13,976	$1,024
GL Nissan Sentra	$1,500	0	$1,500
Checking account	$2,006		$2,006
Savings account	$0		
Retirement funds	$18,060		$18,060
Household items	$3,000		$3,000
Jewelry (rings)	$1,700		$1,700
School loans		-$60,042	($60,042)
Unsecured debt (credit cards)		-$17,316	($17,316)
		Final Net Worth	-$50,068

Tell Me a Story

Your net worth is a snapshot of your financial journey. A snapshot similar to that picture of you and your boo on vacation at the Grand Canyon, smiling on the edge of the cliff. Hopefully, while you were there, you didn't just take one picture during your entire vacation. You took a series of pictures that told the story of your entire trip. Likewise, a series of your net worth numbers throughout time tells the story about your financial journey. And what a story it can tell!

Let's take John and David, for instance. They each, separately, have a net worth of $50,000 right now. If we just looked at this snapshot, it's looks like they are both doing financially the same.

Not so fast.

David was like me. Three years ago, he had a net worth of -$50,000. He realized he had to change his behavior and mindset and made the decision to do so. Through hard work, extra jobs, and living a disciplined life, he paid down his debt and even started investing. He's not where he wants to be yet, but he's making progress toward his financial goal. His net worth is now $50,000.

On the other hand, there's John. John's grandmother passed away two years ago and left him a $300,000 inheritance. After that payout, his net worth was hovering about $250,000 at that time and boy, he was a happy camper. Sadly, because he lacked financial training, he let his emotions lead him about how to handle that windfall of money. It overtook him. He bought several $400 gator shoes, got his family's teeth fixed, bought two luxury cars, went to Vegas a few times to "make it rain," and saw a Hollywood therapist. Now his net worth is $50,000. Whoa! What a drastic change! Personally, I think he should have seen the therapist first and then a financial advisor.

Even though these two lads currently have the same net worth, their trajectories tell a different story. True, John might have had more superficial fun than David, but David is building a foundation to be able to have future exciting experiences that won't bankrupt him or his family.

So, what's your story?

To begin telling your financial story, set the goal to track your net worth at the end of every quarter. There are twelve months in a year and when you group them into four groups, there are three months in each group. Many financial institutions and companies look at their quarterly numbers too. Treat your household as a company and see yourself as the CFO, the chief financial officer. Make it a goal to calculate your net worth on March 31, June 30, September 30, and December 31 of each year. Hopefully, those data points will start telling the story you'll be glad to hear.

Here is a mini net worth sheet. A full printable sheet can be found at CreativeWealthAcademy.net.

Item	Value	- Debt	= Equity
House			
Vehicle			
Cash			
Checking account			
Savings account			
Retirement account			
Household items			
Debt (student loans, credit cards, etc.) (negative amount)			
Total			

Know Your True Worth

"I am not my hair.
I am not this skin . . .
I am the soul that lives within."

India.Arie shot some wisdom our way with this song, but there's one more factor she forgot to list. You are NOT your net worth!

Please understand this.

Your net worth is not an indicator of your worth as a person, a mother, a father, or a friend. It is not an indicator of your ability in your profession.

It is not an indicator of your contribution to society. Sometimes, it is not even a true indicator of your financial capabilities.

For people who took out significant school loans and haven't invested in any significant assets yet, their net worth is extremely low or even in the negative. They might have a basic understanding of finances, but because of school costs, their net worth is much lower than desired. Many Millennials and Gen Xers who were swept away in the student loan tidal wave have experienced this upsetting phenomenon.

This point of not being your net worth is also true on the other side of the spectrum, concerning the wealthy. I dive into this concept in the next section, but it's worth stating here. We make top ten billionaire lists, place people on the covers of magazines, and worship them on these high pedestals because of high net worth. All the while, a lot of these same people suffer from high anxiety if the stock market drops a few points. They don't want to lose their billionaire status. They don't want to be thrown off the "highest net worth" list. They've intertwined their actual *life worth* with their *net worth*.

Big no-no.

If their net worth begins to drop, the view of themselves begins to drop too. This is a correlation you do not want to adopt. I wish I could grab them by the shoulders and emphatically yell, "You are not your financial net worth! You are more than possessions or zeroes and ones in a computer. You are so much more than a number!"

But due to cultural programming, we are conditioned to assign the value of ourselves to the value of our income or, if we know it, our net worth. To avoid this detriment, we need to know that while it is important to be aware of our numbers, they are only a tool to guide us in the right direction to reach our financial goals. They are not an indication of our value and impact in society or our purpose in life.

Mother Teresa probably had a tiny personal net worth—yet what was her worth to the people she cared for? What was her worth to her nation? What was her worth to this world?

But don't forget there are other metrics—such as creativity, contribution, compassion, and mercy—that are far more important to your destiny and purpose in this world. I talk about your financial net worth in this book, but I was recently challenged to see net worth as comprising four separate factors: your health, skill set, influence *and* money. Improving these non-financial areas will, most likely, improve your financial situation as well. Nevertheless, finding out your financial net worth is still an important strategy for you to get your financial journey on track. Now, let's get back to work and lay out all the numbers.

Chapter Six

(Outer Game)
LAY OUT ALL THE NUMBERS

Lay Your Cards on the Table

Now that you have made a decision, listed your reasons, started to set goals, and you know your net worth, it is the time to start devising a game plan.

Clarity brings focus, and focus moves you forward.

So, with moving forward, we are going to lay out all our expenses for the month. These include fixed expenses, variable expenses, debt payments, and even charged-off accounts.

Fixed Expenses

A fixed expense will be the same amount month to month. For example, your rent is a fixed expense within the time of the lease. It won't change from month to month. It stays constant. Other fixed expenses might include your car payments and life insurance or other insurances you have during the length of their contracts. Once a contract is over, it might fluctuate if new terms are brought in. Record your fixed expenses on the provided sheet on CreativeWealthAcademy.net.

Variable Expenses

A variable expense changes from month to month, depending on external factors and internal choices. Some examples of variable expenses are your utilities, which can change depending on your monthly use. If you don't turn off lights and run the air conditioner all day, that expense will be higher than it needs to be. If you're more conservative with energy, then your bill will reflect that. If you eat out every other day, your food expenses will be significantly higher than someone who eats out once or twice a month. The most common variable expenses are food, gas, beauty, and entertainment costs. Karaoke, anyone?

You probably think you have an idea of what these numbers are, especially the fixed expenses, but until you intentionally track them, it will be difficult to see the actual numbers.

When Shayne and I started our financial freedom journey, we immediately began to closely track our variable expenses. That's when I found out we were spending almost $900 a month on food for only two people! What the heck were we eating? Late-night takeout and random trips to the supermarkets were devouring us. We were bleeding out by a thousand papercuts. So, by tracking your variable expenses for a certain amount of time, it can show you where you are bleeding out financially. It will highlight the areas you need to address first and do some major adjustments.

Is it time consuming? Yes. Can it be tedious and boring? Certainly.

But you don't have to do it for a lifetime, and the data you receive from it will be instrumental in guiding your financial plan. I was detailed with my tracking. If Shayne bought a pack of gum, I tracked it. If I got a grande soy Tazo chai latte with an extra shot, I recorded it. When I say everything, I mean everything. I'm only asking you to do it for one to three months (to get averages) but I did it for six years. *Six years!* I was serious about knowing exactly how much money was coming in and exactly where our money was flowing out.

If you asked me, "Genein, how much did you guys spend on food in March 2012?" I would say, "$457.45." "Ok, how much did you spend on gas in October 2013?" I would say, "$193.76."

Bam. It's all there.

Because clarity brings focus, and focus moves you forward.

There's an App for That

When I was tracking my expenses, I saved all my receipts. Every Sunday, I logged them into an Excel spreadsheet that tallied them. Like I mentioned, it was time consuming but worth it.

Now there are amazing apps that make this task so simple. Download a few free apps and go through their platforms. Do you like the layout? Is inputting the amounts easy or cumbersome? As of 2019, my two favorite apps are EveryDollar, recommended by Dave Ramsey, and YNAB (You Need a Budget). Some other cool finance apps are Mint and Clarity Money.

My top choice is EveryDollar, because you can preplan your budget before you get paid and then go through the month and pay all your expenses. At the end of the month, you can compare how your actual spending matched your plan and adjust accordingly. For an extra fee, the app will even link to your bank account to help streamline the tracking process. That's not a necessity, but it's there, if you desire it.

A Quick Sample Personal Budget

Income		
Expenses	Expected	Actual
Giving		
Savings		
Mortgage/rent		
Utilities (gas, water, electric)		
Cable		
Phone		
Food		
Restaurants		
Entertainment		
Childcare		
Insurances		
Health and beauty		
Car payment		
Gas		
Credit cards		
School loans		

"The only man who sticks closer to you in adversity than a friend is a creditor."

—Unknown

Debt Payments

These expenses are what you owe to companies, to banks, and to people. You should have already encountered these numbers when you were calculating your net worth. Debts include car payments, credit cards, student loans, medical bills, and personal loans. And oh, those personal loans. Don't they make family dinners a bit more dramatic?

When recording these numbers, write down the total amount owed, monthly payments, annual percentage rate (APR), and due date. Go to CreativeWealthAcademy.net for these forms.

Charged-Off Accounts

These are never fun. It's like being on a scavenger hunt for sour pickles. These are former debts that companies tried to collect from you but because you were playing hide and go seek, they sold the debt to another company for a fraction of what you owed. Locating these debts is like trying to track down Captain Jack Sparrow and the *Black Pearl*. They can be elusive and frustrating. Here are some tips for contacting your creditors.

A Garnished Surprised

"What?" she cried, exasperated that this was happening. Again.

"Why are my wages being garnished?" Suzanne asked her human resources (HR) supervisor, who was staring at her in disbelief. She couldn't believe that once again this was happening to her. Right when she had begun to get her finances in order and her credit-cards balances lowered, BAM! She got blindsided with a garnishment. Garnishments allow companies to take a part of your paycheck without your permission.

"I don't know," the HR supervisor responded. "This creditor said your account was significantly past due and they received a court order to garnish your wages."

She looked up at Suzanne. "Didn't you see this account on your credit report?"

Suzanne blinked. "Uh, my credit report? I didn't pull my credit report." She looked down at her shoes. "I didn't think I needed to."

Her supervisor smiled at her compassionately. "Well, don't worry. This isn't the end of the world. Go and pull your credit report and make sure you are aware of all the accounts that are on the file. The length of this garnishment is not that long and will be over before you know it!"

"Ok," she responded, still feeling a bit defeated but not as bad. "I'll run my report for anything else I need to settle. Thanks for letting me know about this," she said, as she started back to her desk.

"Bad news isn't wine. It doesn't improve with age."

—Colin Powell

Pulling Your Report

No one likes to be blindsided with bad news. Yet, it can happen, especially when we don't have access to complete information. When dealing with your creditors, pulling your credit report on a regular basis is a must. Not only does it assist you with getting your financial ducks in a row, but it can also alert you to any suspicious activity, which could escalate into identity (ID) theft.

I've ridden that scary roller coaster and trust me; ID theft is no exciting ride. I go more into that in chapter twenty-eight.

There are three credit reporting agencies that will provide you one free credit report a year. Scheduling an annual time when you pull your report is good, because it becomes of part of your financial routine. New Year's Day or at the end of a financial quarter can be a good time. How about your birthday or an anniversary? Choose a date you'll remember and stick to it. But for this moment, pulling your credit report as you gather all your credit accounts together is necessary. You don't want any unwelcome surprises and you certainly don't want a "Congratulations! Your wages are now being garnished!" announcement!

You can order the reports online by visiting annualcreditreport.com or calling 1-877-322-8228. You will need to provide your name, current and former addresses, Social Security number, and date of birth to verify your identity. It's a good idea to list all your previous addresses and employers in a secure place for easy access each time you do this.

Make Contact

The most obvious way to get the information about your creditors is to locate your more recent paper bills and pull the numbers from those documents. If you chose to go green, then they're online.

Stay Organized

I keep saying it. Clarity brings focus, and focus moves you forward. If your bills are in one place and organized, it's easier to handle them. Ditch the piles of papers all over the office. They are chaotic and stressful. Keep an accordion folder or a filing system. That overwhelming feeling will start to dissipate.

For my financial paper documents, I have an accordion folder with these sections.

Sections

1. Recent Documents (to be filed)
2. Donations (tax write-offs)
3. Car Documents
4. Debts (student loans, credit cards, credit reports)
5. Insurances
6. Medical Documents
7. Utilities

8. Paystubs
9. Savings/Investments
10. Banking
11. Tax Documents (dues, conferences)
12. Living Trust, Wills, Life Insurance Instructions

This are the sections I needed for my life and profession. You might need other sections. I clear this folder out at the end of December and put aside what I will need for tax day. I then begin the new year with a clean folder.

For your computer, if you use one particular browser, create a folder in your bookmark section and label it "Bills." You can keep all the Web addresses of the billing companies in one place. Keep utilities together, credit cards together, banks together, and insurances together. Keep it clean. Keep it simple.

Now, it's time to make contact.

Be Confident, But Not Mean
Be Sensible, But Not Bullied

Right now, you're just getting all your numbers together. You're not haggling with creditors and working out deals just yet. You need to see all your numbers, in black and white, in front of you. Hopefully, this information is all online, but if you have charged-off accounts or extremely past-due accounts, the companies might forbid you from online access. This forces you to call them.

That's when you put your game face on.

Before you call them, be prepared. Have your identifying numbers ready. These are the account number, your Social Security number, and any passwords the company might ask you. If you are not prepared when you call, it is easier to become frazzled and unable to stand your ground.

"Hi, this is Genein Letford, and I am calling to get some basic information about my account."

That's how you lead in. If your account is past due, the person on the phone is going to do what he or she can to get you to make a payment right then and there. That's their job. They are trained to do this. They are trained to get under your skin, and boy are they good. If they have a script to get you to pay, you need a script to maintain control and follow your financial plan.

Your first tool is the broken record. If you were born in the 1980s or earlier, you might remember a large, black, Frisbee-like disc that had the ability to play music when placed on a contraption bearing a needle. That item was called a record player and that black disc was called a record. For many of my younger readers, you might haven't the slightest clue as to what I'm talking about. No worries! Feel free to look it up online.

In the late 1980s, while my sister and I were singing to our records, "Puff the Magic Dragon" was our personal favorite. After months of pure enjoyment of this soundtrack, the record got a scratch on it. This caused the music to skip and repeat the same line over and over and over again. Puff, our magic dragon, suddenly turned into a rapping lizard!

"Puff the magic—Puff the magic—Puff the magic dragon lived by the sea, by the sea, sea, sea, sea!"

It was annoying for us, but that move is critical for you.

This is what you do while you're on the phone. Play your broken record.

When the customer service rep starts to badger you, just repeat the lines over and over again.

"I am calling for information about my account. I need to know my balance, my APR, the minimum payment, and what I need to do to bring my account current."

Hopefully, they will hear the kind determination in your voice and give you this information. If they start to push you into making a payment, just respond, "Thank you so much for this information. I am currently creating a plan to pay off this debt and once that plan is in place, I will be sending in a payment and working on bringing this account current. So once again, I need to know my balance, my APR, the minimum payment, and what I need to do to bring my account current."

Not wanting you to get off the phone without making a payment, they'll come at you with this, "Well, if you don't make a payment today, your credit score will continue to drop."

They might even come at you with having someone take your house or your first-born child. In the past, they have said some crazy things! Gladly, it is against the law to harass debt clients. They shouldn't be calling after a certain time in the evening and certainly shouldn't be threatening you. But if you don't know your rights, they might take advantage of you.

You must know your rights as a consumer.

If they start to harass you, just repeat, "Once again, I thank you for your help. I need to know my balance, my APR, the minimum payment, and what I need to do to bring my account current."

Be the broken record. It works.

Lower Your Interest Rate

By receiving information about your account status, balance, and interest rate, you are collecting data to win this game. But strategy is also key. As long as your interest rate is sky high, your balance is possibly still going up every month. When you call to collect data, attempt to receive a lower interest rate. Here's how to accomplish this.

Collect the account information. Inform the credit provider that you are committed to becoming debt free and you would like to lower your interest rate. Claim that other cards are offering rates at half their rate. Ask them to lower your rate by 50 percent or 40 percent.

If they deny you, remind them that you have other options to transfer the balance to other cards that have a lower rate. Remind them that you have been loyal customer for X years and you prefer not to switch, but you will if they cannot lower your rate. Rinse and repeat.

This short call could save you thousands of dollars and speed up your debt payoff journey.

"When you know better, you do better."

—Maya Angelou

Once you have all your debt numbers, fixed and variable expenses, fill in the worksheet at creativewealthacademy.net. Look at it. Stare at it. Speak to it. Say this: "These are my numbers for right now, but this is not my destiny. These numbers are here because of my past choices, but I have made the decision to do better, now that I know better."

Your numbers will go where you decide to take them. Genae, my sister, came to this realization and attacked the monsters in her closet. She now is in a much better place financially.

Ready for the next step? Great! It's time to see what type of shovel you're working with. Shovel? Why do I need a shovel?" you might ask. Well, to get out of a bad situation, you have to do more than make a decision and clarify your numbers. You have to get a shovel to dig yourself out of the negative. This financial shovel is also known as your income streams. This will be the tool, the cash flow, you need to climb out of the debt you're in and head into the financial freedom you're destined for.

Chapter Seven

(Outer Game)
WHAT'S YOUR
CASH FLOW?

Cash Flow: The Real Game of Life

"Does everyone have an occupation card?" I asked my students, as they passed out the playing cards to their teams.

"Yep!" replied Diego. "I'm a plumber!" He laughed his hearty laugh that always put a smile on my face. "I have a whopping $2,500 monthly income."

"What's your job?" Diego looked at his neighbor, Frank, who was filling out his sheet.

"I'm an airline pilot!" he waved his card. "Whoa! I'm making $9,000 a month!" A supportive rumble rustled throughout the classroom.

Every winter and summer break, I gather students from Alumni360, my teen mentorship group, to play the CASHFLOW game, created by *Rich Dad Poor Dad* author Robert Kiyosaki. This group of amazing sixth through twelfth graders meets once a month to learn financial literacy, collegiate planning, and life skills.

I love CASHFLOW! This game not only gives them a heads-up about expenses, passive income, and finding opportunities, but it also makes them aware that people with average incomes can become financially independent sooner than they think.

"Frank," I looked at him, "that's a nice income," I slowed my speech, "but what are your monthly expenses?"

He scanned his sheet and gasped. "Whoa, $8,800! That's kinda high!"

We meet eyes and my eyebrows raise. Turning my attention to Diego, I ask, "And what are your monthly expenses, Mr. Plumber?"

He glances at his card. "Hmmm, it says here my expenses are $2,000."

"Ok. So, what's your cash flow?" I asked him, hoping he still had his mental math skills he learned in elementary school.

"It's, let's see, $500!" he exclaimed, scribbling the number on his financial sheet.

"And Frank, what is your cash flow?"

"It's only $200!" he looked bewildered. "Why is my cash flow so low?" he asked.

"Well, Frank, the fact that it is a positive number is a good thing. But in working-class, middle-class America, the more money people make, the more they spend." I stopped to carefully scan the class. "Actually, many people have a *negative* cash flow."

"How can you make your cash flow negative?" Lizeth asked from the next table over. She was eavesdropping the whole time.

"Easy. You spend more money than you make," Antonio, my senior student piped in. All the heads bobbed up and down in unison.

"Trust me," I added, "it's more common than you think."

What's Your Cash Flow?

Similar to your net worth, knowing your cash flow is just as an important. Like net worth, it's a number that many of us didn't even know we should be looking for. Also like net worth, it's easy to calculate.

Your cash flow is the amount of money flowing into your household that isn't allocated toward any expense. Basically, it's the money left after all your bills are paid and savings and living expenses have been taken out. With the plight of many Americans today, who are living paycheck to paycheck, most people's cash flow is zero. And now, with the advent of credit cards and payday loans, many people are living with a cash flow that's in the negative, sending out more money a month than is flowing in.

There are many reasons people might have a negative cash flow. Economic factors, low wages, and the job market are a few but, in many cases, it's our personal habits. We don't understand Parkinson's Law, which states, "Expenses will always rise in direct proportion to income." Basically, the more money we make, the more money we spend. We celebrate a $300 raise with a $400 car payment!

To tackle our debt and be in a position to build wealth, we will have to be intentional with increasing our cash flow and sending it to the right places. Our income is our most efficient tool for building wealth, and if it is being eaten up by tons of bills and undisciplined behavior, it's difficult to move the needle in the right direction. Cash flow is also affected by your creativity. Section eight does a deeper dive on how increasing your creative health can also increase your financial wealth. Your financial prosperity is encased within your creative ideas: it's all connected.

So, once your bills are clearly laid out, identifying and increasing your cash flow is your next step. There are two ways to make this happen: lower your expenses and/or increase your income. Simple concept, yes—but it takes effort, creativity, and strategic planning to implement. Let's take a look at your spending plan—also known as the budget!

Section Two Summary

1. The numbers might look scary, but look at them as challenges or a game to remove debilitating fear.

2. Calculate your financial net worth.

3. Understand that your net worth is *not* your worth as a person.

4. Lay out all the numbers, including debt, income, and expenses. Contact creditors.

5. Determine your cash flow and focus on increasing it.

Section Three
BUSTING OUT A BUDGET

Chapter Eight

(Outer Game)
BUDGETING
THE BUDGET

*"If your outgo exceeds your income, then your
upkeep will be your downfall."*

—BILL EARLE

Expenses: How Low Can You Go?

Meet Claudia. She's twenty-seven years old and is ok with gazing into people's mouths as a dental assistant at a high-end dental practice. She is your typical American, financially speaking, with loads of debt and no spending plan or goals. She has $10,000 in student loans, $2,000 on three combined credit cards, regular household expenses, and is operating with a -$200 cash flow. This means she's spending $200 more a month than she's bringing in.

This is Claudia and she needs your help.

Look at her budget and advise her which areas she should cut back on or totally eliminate. Her goal is to (1) bring her cash flow into the positive and (2) increase her cash flow as much as possible without reducing her social life to living in a cave throwing pebbles at a volleyball named Wilson.

Claudia's Expenses

Monthly Expenses	Monthly Cost	Budget Savings
Rent	$1,000	
Utilities	$100	
Cable TV	$100	
Internet	$75	
Home phone	$50	
Cell phone	$90	
Car insurance	$125	
Credit card payments	$300	
Groceries/household	$350	
Gas	$250	
Newspaper subscription	$25	
Coffee shop	$150	
Netflix subscription	$15	
Gym membership	$65	
Hair salon	$150	
Restaurants	$400	
Tithe/Charity	$320	
Totals	**$3,565**	$

* Which items did you decide to eliminate?
* Which items did you allow her to keep at a lower amount?
* Are you letting her sustain her coffee fix?
* Can she keep watching *This Is Us* on cable?
* How about that weekly newspaper?

Look back at all your modifications on her expenses and think about the reasons that caused you to make those changes.

Here are the areas my Creative Wealth Academy seminar students address when they meet Claudia.

1. She can eliminate her newspaper subscription and read the news on her phone.
2. She can get rid of her cable and use Netflix as it is a cheaper option.
3. She can make coffee at home and lower her Starbucks outings.
4. She can purchase running shoes and allow outside trails to be her gym.
5. She can cook more meals at home.

Regulate the Fun: Don't Eliminate It

When we get excited about casting the vision of being debt free and deciding to have success in this area, we might go to the extreme and cut out any and everything that is not an essential for survival. No restaurants. No entertainment. No fun whatsoever!

Good luck with that!

This initial reaction is not surprising, given your enthusiasm to become financially free. Nevertheless, these types of modifications are dangerous, because they are unsustainable. Cutting out *all* fun (going out to eat, to the movies, Starbucks, or whatever else you would put in this category) will not last long. You'll get frustrated and give up.

We don't want that!

So instead of eliminating these enjoyments completely, regulate them with intention and move them to the "rewards" section.

For instance, before your beloved "decision day," you were buying a double mocha cartwheel latte with a triple shot of caffeine and an extra layer of whipped cream alongside a ham and cheese croissant. Wow, that's a mouthful! The total of this delicious daily order is about $9.75, which puts your Starbucks bill at a whopping $195 a month! It's funny that so many of us are putting more money into our coffee habit than our retirement!

I'm not a big coffee drinker, but I am guilty of getting a yummy breakfast sandwich and a $2.45 tea (which is the same price as a whole box of tea bags). Once Shayne and I decided to become debt free, I moved these nonessential Starbucks purchases to fun Fridays! If I had a good week and achieved my financial, personal, and professional goals for that week, I enjoyed Starbucks on Friday. I savored that experience, because it was well earned. It was no longer an unconscious purchase or an entitled event but a treasured reward experience. I looked forward to it. Hmmm ... pure heaven.

Restaurants and going out had the same treatment. Now, we didn't eliminate our restaurant budget entirely, but we did lower it substantially. Our restaurant/entertainment budget allowed us to go out once every two weeks instead of twice in one week.

Because we like to eat and have adventures, if we reached a milestone with our debt, we celebrated! Paying off Shayne's car was cause for a celebratory mini trip to San Diego. We still used financial wisdom and found the best deals, but we took the time to celebrate that win. When we paid off all our credit cards, I got a massage and Shayne did an activity he enjoyed.

You've got to celebrate your wins! Your brain needs to experience rewards to keep your motivation strong. In chapter eighteen, we'll talk about chunking your debt together, so you have your milestones already established. So, no need to eliminate *all* the fun; modify it and regulate it to the "rewards zone." Let the fun serve you, instead of you being a slave to it.

Now, let's investigate ways to patch leaking money holes in your cash flow.

Chapter Nine

(Outer Game)
LET'S MAKE A DEAL:
BUDGET BUSTERS
AND BLESSINGS

Don't Set It and Forget It

"Hi, I'm calling about my phone bill. It seems a bit high," I told the AT&T representative, who was slowly pulling up my account. Even though they're a multimillion-dollar company, their computers are as slow as molasses. "Can I qualify for a teacher discount" I asked.

"Ok. Well, I'll be happy to check into that for you," he responded. After he went over my bill to see if I qualified for the teacher discount, reluctantly he said, "I'm sorry about this, but you don't qualify for the discount because you're not in a large district."

Really? That doesn't make any sense! I'm still a teacher!

"Oh, ok," I responded nicely. "Well, I think Verizon has a program that is still more affordable for my needs. Because I'm out of contract, I'll try them. Thank you for your time."

"Oh, Ms. Letford!" he hurriedly called out, hoping I didn't hang up the phone, "Yes, you are out of contract, I see. It also looks like your husband will be out of contract soon. We have special pricing for our out-of-contract customers!"

"Oh, you do?" I cautiously responded.

He proceeded to inform me that my bill could be cut almost in half because of us being out of contract, along with some other factors we were unaware of.

That day I learned a valuable lesson.

Don't set it and forget it!

Don't just keep paying your installment bills without challenging the idea that you are getting the best price! Remember, to increase your cash flow, lowering your expenses is a big section of that goal. If you're overpaying by twenty dollars on five of your bills, those high payments are eating a big chunk—$100!—of your cash-flow power.

Here are some tips that will assist you in getting the biggest bang for your buck.

Check Rates Annually

Because you have all your expenses clearly laid out, it should be a simple process to call each of them to check if you are getting the best deal. We do this on an annual or biannual basis. My husband would call our internet provider and, more often than not, the rep would inform him of a deal for services we already were using. Be mindful though, and don't get tricked and sign up for additional services if you do not absolutely need them. Still, companies will host promotions throughout the year and sometimes you might qualify. You might even want to shop around beforehand and check the rates of competitors to use as leverage during negotiations.

Areas to employ these tactics include phone bills, cable/internet bills, car insurance, renters/home insurance, and any other area that's a recurring payment.

You have power—but only if you choose to use it effectively. The company's goals are to keep you as a customer at the highest price point you can pay. Most likely, no one will call you to offer you a better deal. You have to be proactive and seek out those promotions. Be your own advocate.

Debt Discussion

Debt is depressing. Debilitating debt is suffocating and for some, debt is death. Even though I have never felt suicidal over my debt, many people have. Lost futures and broken families have been left in their wake.

The Bible says, "The borrower is slave to the lender" (Proverbs 22:7, NIV). I have felt this firsthand.

The weight of our enslavement chains to our Bank of America credit card was heavy. The interest was $161 with a total payment of $250. I knew my numbers. I knew the APR (27 percent), the monthly payments ($250), and the total amount owed ($8,220). What I didn't know was how to relieve the stress of this bill.

So instead of hiding the Bank of America bill or trying to stay afloat month to month with paying an exorbitant interest fee, I put my pride aside and called them.

"Hi, thank you for calling Bank of America. This is Dave, how can I help you?" a chipper male voice greeted me. Do they have voice classes to learn how to sound overly cheerful on the phone?

"Hi, Dave. I seem to be in a bind. My bill is way too high for us to handle right now. We're paying $161 in interest alone. That's quite alarming. I really don't want to stop paying what we owe, and I don't want the account to be charged-off, but we can't keep this up." The stress in my voice was becoming more evident as I kept talking. *Stay cool, Genein, stay cool!* I thought.

I continued.

"Are there any modifications you can make to our bill so there's not so much interest?"

"Well, I'm sorry to hear you're having trouble making your payment," He actually sounded sincere. "We actually do have a debt assistance program. If you qualify for this program, it will lower your monthly payment, stop all over-the-limit fees, and reduce your interest rate from 27 percent to 4.5 percent," he said.

Wow! How do I sign up for this?! Do I have to tap dance? Sign away the birthrights to my first child? What do I have to do? Tell me now! I think. I take in a deep breath.

"That's sounds great," I responded calmly. "How can we qualify for the program?"

"To qualify, you have to make three on-time payments and then you can be enrolled," he added.

Ok, I thought, *I can do this. It will be tight, but it will be worth it if all those benefits are actually true.*

"Ok, David. I think we can make that happen. I will contact you in three months after three on-time payments to sign up. Thank you so much for your time." I know he told me his name was Dave, but I'm assuming his birth name is David. If his mama named him David, I'm going to call him David.

Once again, these breaks don't just fall in your lap. They won't hit you in the face. You have to be proactive and diligently seek them out. Bank of America would have been just fine with me paying the minimum payment until the good Lord called me home. Debt payments are set up for just that.

You are the stock market they're investing in. At 27 percent interest, they are getting a wonderful return on *your money!* Without this program, and only paying the minimum amount, we would have been paying this account for several more years and giving them thousands upon thousands of dollars in interest. Bank of America would have been just fine with that decision. Just fine.

Discounts for Being You

You know the old adage, "A penny saved is a penny earned." This is still true. When expenses go down, it's like you just got a raise! As you're working on increasing your cash flow and paying off debt, those pennies add up. The more pennies you're able to keep in your pocket to reach your financial goals, the better. When my husband and I made our decision to become debt free, we looked at ourselves and our demographic information in a whole new way.

+ Do they offer any discounts for teachers?
+ Do they offer any discounts for students? (I was a part-time master's student.)
+ Are there any American Automobile Association (AAA) discounts?
+ Any discounts for cute couples?
+ How about karaoke singers?

You won't know if you don't ask!

I presented these questions to our service providers, and it worked! To lower my husband's car insurance premium, I added myself as a qualified driver. Because I had a teaching credential and a good student qualification, the company took almost thirty dollars off our monthly bill! Score!

If you serve or have served in the armed forces, offer that information to the companies. If you are a senior citizen or have an American Association of Retired Persons (AARP) card, ask to see if they recognize those discounts. Hey, even if it's your birthday, let them know!

I used to say, "The only birthdays that matter are sixteen, 'cause you're sweet; twenty-one, 'cause you're legal; and sixty-five, 'cause you get to eat at Denny's for half price!" So, enjoy those milestone birthdays and get those discounts!

Coupons and Club Cards

Watching the show *The Coupon Clippers* was astonishing and impressive. Yet most people don't have the tenacity nor the time to truly master the world of clipping, stacking, and utilizing coupons effectively. During the time of our intense debt-reduction period, I was an intense coupon clipper. I monitored the prices of items we purchased regularly and bought them in bulk when they were at their rock-bottom price. I would also shop at multiple stores, a grocery store, and Target, to ensure I was getting the best deal. I'm not going to lie, this took a significant amount of time and until I got into a rhythm, it also took a great deal of mental capacity. I highly recommend *The Everything Couponing Book*, if this is an area you want to excel in. I saved almost $2,000 a year by effectively employing these techniques.

Honey is also a really great browser extension you can use for online coupons and promo codes. You can save so much money, and it's free! Check out www.joinhoney.com to find automatic promo codes, coupons, and deals.

If running after fifty-cent and one-dollar coupons doesn't excite you like it did me, that's fine. I still urge you to be aware of the easiest form of using coupons for big items. For instance, if you shop at Bed Bath and Beyond or Buy Buy Baby (BBB), having a 20 percent off coupon in your hand is a must. Why? Those coupons are ubiquitous! They're everywhere! They come in the mail, in your email, and some are lying on the ground right in front of the store! I honestly think it should be against the law to walk into BBB empty-handed! I wonder if Bed Bath and Beyond intentionally hikes their prices up 20 percent just because of the ubiquity of these coupons.

Don't neglect those grocery store loyalty cards. Once I was shopping with my uncle, and we needed to get some items from our local supermarket. Many supermarkets have free loyalty cards, which allow you to pay the loyalty-card price. My uncle never felt the need to sign up for these and after our items were scanned in, the cashier asked him if he had one.

"Nope," he responded, as if it was a bother. I frantically reached into my bag to grab my keys, "Wait, I have one!" and gave it to the cashier. Being a thrifty shopper, I couldn't stand by and watch him pay a higher amount than necessary!

His eyes were glued to the monitor as all the excess charges were being wiped away.

"Wow!" he gasped. The discount came to about $20 less than his original bill. All that from a tiny card!

He was sold. He signed up for a card on the spot.

Like taxes, pay your fair share, but don't pay any more than you have to! You're burning your hard-earned money if you do.

Another place to use coupons easily is office supply stores, like Staples, OfficeMax, and Office Depot. Let's face it—ink and paper are expensive. Whichever store you frequent, get on their mailing list, and save those coupons they send you. You can save an impressive amount on big-ticket items just by giving them a piece of paper—a coupon.

We buy our paper in reams of ten that normally cost fifty dollars for one box. But after I send in the rebate, we end up paying only ten dollars for ten reams. That's one dollar for a ream of paper! It only took about four minutes to fill out the rebate form online. Be intentional to keep as many pennies in your pocket! Then send those extra pennies to your debt!

Once again, only use coupons on things you *actually need* and use. Don't save coupons on items you don't need, because you just end up spending more money. That defeats the purpose of saving your pennies to reduce your debt. Be intentional and be disciplined.

Chapter Ten

(Outer Game)
NEGOTIATING: A LOST AMERICAN ART

The Negotiator

"How much is this?" I asked, pointing to a turquoise green turtle hanging on for dear life at the end of a black lanyard.

"It's fifteen dollars, but for you," he replied, as he smiled slyly in my direction, "I can give it to you for ten dollars. You seem like a nice girl."

I squinted my eyes, thinking, *Flattery will get you nowhere, mister!*

I picked up the necklace and the turtle's eyes connected with mine. I couldn't leave Costa Rica without a trinket to remind me of this outrageous trip. But I couldn't let him see my growing desire for this item. I needed to negotiate.

"Oh, well, thank you. But I was thinking this would be about five dollars." I glanced back up at him. "Could you make that work?"

"Oh, I don't know," he responded, as I started to place the little turtle back into his resting place on the cloth. I smiled and started to turn away.

"Wait!"

I stopped.

"How about eight dollars? I can let him go for eight," he assured me.

I glanced down at the turtle, who seemed to be enjoying this whole back-and-forth banter over him, and then I returned my gaze to the man.

"Ok, that's seems all right," I responded, digging through my Pura Vida bag for money. With a beautiful turquoise turtle around my neck, I walked away, silently celebrating my win.

Haggle

In other countries, negotiating is the norm. Some street vendors even consider it rude if you don't haggle with them. It's like going to a football game and facing the wrong direction. Why even be there? Negotiating is a part of the experience.

But in the US, we haven't really adopted that process into our purchasing rituals. We see a price, and we either pay it or we don't. There are many places, like supermarkets and chain stores in the mall that do not negotiate (though some kiosk businesses do)! But sadly, we take this form of strict purchasing over into areas where we could negotiate, but we never attempt to challenge the listed price.

This actually occurred for me not too long ago. I needed a medical procedure done that wasn't covered by my insurance. My husband looked at the financial payment plan and unexpectedly asked, "Is there any way to have a discount on this price?"

The nurse looked at him and raised her eyebrows. "You know what, let me ask the doctor." She then came back and said he would be willing to give us a 20 percent discount—a savings of almost $1,000! Just by asking a simple little question!

Not knowing when to negotiate and how to negotiate can be costly. A friend of mine, who had no car-buying experience, sauntered onto a car lot, and ended up being taken to the bank! That's a saying for "he was hoodwinked!" He found the car he adored and instead of haggling with the car salesperson, he assumed the price plastered on the window was the price he was supposed to pay!

"Why didn't you negotiate with him?" I inquired, honestly wondering which planet he abandoned to come here, completely unprepared. Who doesn't negotiate on a car lot? That's the ONE place most Americans know to haggle.

"I just didn't know I could," he responded with his shoulders shrugged. "I thought the price you see is the price you pay."

He didn't know. He just didn't know.

Ladies and gentlemen, ignorance is costly. Not knowing comes at a high price.

This isn't a book about effective negotiating (check my website for my powerful negotiating course) but I do highly suggest you learn the strategies of negotiation before you attempt it. Do not go in empty-handed, unprepared, and emotional.

Negotiating is another form of being creative. Being able to look at a situation from multiple perspectives, discern the motivating factors of the other person and connect the unconnected are all creative problem-solving skills. This is another reason why creative training is a benefit to overall life success, in finances and beyond.

Know your numbers, know the worth of the item or the worth of your value, and know the psychological strategies that will lead the transaction in your favor. Know you can walk away if the situation doesn't meet your minimum standards. Minimal research in this area could potentially save you thousands of dollars. Thousands!

Negotiating Women

As women, we lose thousands of dollars because of this lack of negotiating skills. It's interesting that women are better advocates and negotiators for everyone except themselves. We will negotiate for our children and advocate hard for those facing injustice, but when it comes to our own well-being, we shrink into the shadows of unworthiness.

Why?

Do we not know our own worth?

When we don't take the time to learn how to negotiate, our salaries and other professional benefits will suffer; and those losses accumulate. For instance, I could take a job for $50,000, but had I been trained to negotiate, I could have raised my pay to $55,000. Over ten years, I would have earned a total of $50,000 more in salary, all because I exercised the skill of negotiation.

We don't think about the *accumulation of disadvantages*—meaning that over time, those losses add up. This is why I teach an online course on negotiation in my Creative Wealth Academy on how to improve your ability of getting paid for your skills, talents, and contributions in the workplace. Everyone should invest in improving their negotiation skills, but women really need to pay attention to this skill, especially women of color.

Learning how to negotiate is basically learning how to interact with people and leverage opportunities in your favor. But to leverage opportunities, you first must be able to recognize them.

Chapter Eleven

(Outer Game) RECOGNIZING OPPORTUNITY

Recognizing the Open Door

"fdjklfajkdfjkajskfjkdl" "Genein"
"jflajkldjfkjdkajfkjdsklajfd"

Have you ever been in a crowded room with tons of people chattering and suddenly you hear your name as clearly as if there was only one person in the room? This happens quite often. Why is it difficult to hear the multiple conversations around you, but your name is clearly detected? It's because your name is the most beautiful sound to your mind. Your brain has set up filters to automatically detect it whenever it is said. It's like Beyoncé on stage at the Grammys. Even if you wanted to ignore your name, you can't.

This happens because of your reticular activating system (RAS). There is so much going on around you all the time; from birds chirping, coffee machines grinding, people laughing, and even that squirrel who's trying to play Frogger just to get across the street. The activity of the world never stops. If your brain tried to process all that is going on around you with all your senses, it would explode. There's too much stimuli in action. So, to not have a nervous breakdown, your brain has to be selective as to what it allows in and what it must ignore.

Well, Genein, that's a fun science fact, but what does this have to do with my cash flow and finances?

Everything.

It has *everything* to do with your finances.

Before my D-Day (the day I was crying on the floor and made a decision to live a better financial life—my Decision Day), Shayne and I were just bumping along on the road of life, not really cognizant of any financial pitfalls or benefits around us. We were unaware and uninformed.

Once our mindset changed, we started to become more aware of the factors that involve financial success. We prayed to be more open to ideas and opportunities that could lower our expenses and increase our income, therefore increasing our cash flow. We finally—and intentionally—opened our eyes. Our RAS went to work to locate opportunities that we could harness. We were blessed to have some interesting events come our way.

Managing the Night

"BEEP—BEEP—BEEP—BEEP," the shrieking emergency exit door alarm was wailing yet again. I turned my head slowly to look at the clock. Five a.m. NOOOO! This alarm was interrupting a rather pleasant dream I was just getting into.

"Ahhh! This is *not* happening!" my husband whispered under his breath as he hopped out of bed. I just turned my body toward the wall and placed the pillow over my ears.

Grabbing his cell phone, Shayne ran to open the front door just in time to catch a glimpse of the hallway door closing as the perpetrator ran out the emergency exit, setting off the alarm.

"Are you calling the night manager?" I yelled toward the family room where Shayne was angrily pacing, his phone glued to his ear.

"He's not picking up the phone," he responded. "Why do we call him the night manager when he *manages* nothing?!"

Chuckling, I rolled over, begging God for one more hour of sleep. Of course, that was a prayer that went unanswered.

When the day manager finally arrived in her office—two hours later—my husband and I quickly bounded down the stairs to speak to her.

"Vicki, we enjoy living here," Shayne started. I rolled my eyes slightly as if to say, "Not really but because we were working on paying off our debt, it was the best we could afford."

Shayne continued. "But the alarm constantly being set off is starting to upset us. The night manager doesn't pick up his phone, so we're stuck listening to that annoying sound for hours," Shayne informed her, trying to lower the agitation in his voice, trying to sound as professional as possible.

"You two aren't the first to complain about the night manager." She looked beat, like she'd heard this before. The wrinkles on her face tightened and then suddenly loosened. She looked at us, squinting her eyes with the corners of her lips slightly inching up.

"Shayne, you work at night, right?" she asked him. He nodded. He has his own professional branding business, Letford Media, so websites, logos, and media packages can be created at any time, day or night.

"What would you say to taking over the night manager position? There's not much to it. Just lock up the laundry rooms, ticket any illegally parked cars, and turn off any door alarms that go off," she told us. "There's no pay." She raised her eyebrows. "But there is a rent reduction."

Rent reduction? *Whaaaat?*

When she said rent reduction, we were all ears. Our RAS was cued and ready to listen.

After all was said and done, it was a major factor in our debt-reduction plan. When we were first married, our rent was suffocating us with being almost half our take-home income. Shayne had quit his full-time job to start his home business. So, our rent was an expense we had to adjust quickly. Once we made our financial decision to be better stewards of our finances, we then moved to this cheaper location, which brought our rent down to $1,000 a month. Now, with the night manager discount, our rent eventually made it down to $600 a month for a two-bedroom, one-bath apartment in the San Fernando Valley, about 20 miles north of Los Angeles. What a crazy unexpected blessing!

Though this was a wonderful financial blessing, Shayne still worked hard as the night manager. Because he was detailed and meticulous, he earned the respect of the manager and the corporate offices. Yes, he had to enforce the parking rules and eventually tow a couple of cars. This never adds cool points with the tenants, but he was patient with them.

Oh, the stories! One night a recreational vehicle (RV) exploded right next to our window—it was really on fire—and the fire department had to be dispatched. Another night he had to climb through a tenants' window because they locked themselves out. Constantly, in the middle of the night, Shayne would attend to random requests of the tenants who seemed to be lacking the most basic life skills.

On the flip side, he even used the position as a community service outreach. To curb the kids from playing soccer around the parked cars, he launched an unofficial soccer club with the local kids by taking them to a nearby park to play the game. He stretched this night manager position into a mentorship position. Not only was he a positive force in the complex, but we saved almost $11,000 in rent from this unexpected, yet recognized, opportunity.

Be open to unconventional ways to lower your expenses. Lowered expenses are an automatic income raise! Let your RAS spot different ways to get you closer to your debt-reduction goals.

Section Three Summary

1. Look at your expenses and identify expenses that can moved to the rewards section.
2. Reward yourself when you meet your payoff goals.
3. Contact your reoccurring bill companies to ensure you are receiving the best deals.
4. Contact your creditors to see if there are any debt-relief programs.
5. Ask for discounts for your demographics (student, professional, AAA, veteran, etc.).
6. Negotiate your salary, your benefits, and other financial transactions.
7. Be aware of financial debt-reduction opportunities in plain sight. Pay attention!

Let's take a break from the external numbers and dive into the internal game that can be the cause of such high expenses. We'll get back to attacking your debt after these inner game messages!

SEARCHING FOR SUCCESS

Chapter Twelve

(Inner Game)
THE TRUE
VALUE DEAL

The sound of low rumbling planes acted as background noise while we celebrated my little brother's birthday. He'd been infatuated with planes since he was a child, so my mother decided to have his birthday dinner at a swanky restaurant at the Los Angeles (LAX) airport.

Laughing at some old memories, we walked out to the valet to get our cars and head on home. The valet attendant, an older man resembling Morgan Freeman, ran up to my mother to take her ticket. "I'll be right back with your car, ma'am," he politely said to her.

Pulling up in her Lexus, he opened the door as she got in. My brother hopped in the passenger side. She looked at us smiling and drove off.

Turning his attention to my twin sister, he then took her ticket and scurried away. He drove up in her sleek gray Infiniti, and he smiled at Genae as she slid a tip into his hand. "Bye, Nein," she said, as she tossed a glance over her shoulder in my direction and drove off.

There I was, standing alone.

"Last, but certainly not least," he assured me. Fumbling for my valet ticket, it finally revealed itself in a side pocket.

"Oops, here it is," I said, as I handed it to him. I pointed to where I saw my vehicle, "It's the beauty right over there." He looked in the direction I was pointing and headed in that direction.

After a few minutes, he drove up in my car—a 1999 maroon Nissan Sentra. This was a special car. The paint on the roof and hood looked like it had leprosy—speckles and everything. The rear bumper, which was held on to dear life by a black lanyard, needed extra support; packing tape was the current adhesive of choice. Even though the exterior was not pleasing to the eye, the engine was pristine. Her calming purr greeted me as he pulled up.

He got out slowly, looking at the hood of the car and then back at me. He then brought his eyes to meet mine. "You know," he started, carefully choosing his words, "if you just stay in school, you're gonna make it too."

The words hung in the air as he offered me an encouraging smile.

I didn't know what to say. I was at loss for words, so I just sweetly grinned at him, nodding.

"I will," I responded, reassuring him while slipping a tip into his hand. I chuckled to myself. The fact is, I have stayed in school—multiple times. I graduated from the University of California, Los Angeles (UCLA) in psychology, from California State University, Northridge (CSUN) with a master's degree in education, and from Light University with my financial coaching certification. The one thing I knew how to do was stay in school.

Glancing in my rearview mirror, I noticed him watching me as I drove away. I laughed out loud. I then called my mother.

"Mom!" I exclaimed after she answered. "You'll never guess what the valet guy just told me."

I explained to her what happened; she belted out a booming laugh. After catching her breath, she managed to say, "See, Genein, I keep telling you to get a new car!"

How Do *You* Spell Success?

Have you ever stopped to think about the idea of what it means to be successful? Or even more so, have you ever stopped to really contemplate what success means to you? Does having a nice car mean you're successful? A big house?

People who don't take the time to identify the exact definition of success for their own lives will automatically assume society's definition. That definition is usually expensive, materialistic, and often unattainable.

When I was in high school, society's definition of success was what I held onto, right along with the checklist that came with it. The checklist was along these lines.

American Society's List of Success

+ Get a good education from a popular or well-branded school. (Even if it is out of your price range or isn't a true fit for you.)

+ Graduate and find a high-paying job. (Even if you hate going to that job, like 70 percent of Americans today, or have no passion for the work!)

+ Purchase a really expensive car. (Even if you have to stretch the loan to five to seven years so that you can actually *afford* the monthly car payment!)

+ Buy a really big house with extra rooms. (Even if it's just two of you and you never use the extra space.)

+ Have an ultrathin body type at all costs. (Even if it means doing harm to your body.)

+ Buy and consistently upgrade the latest gadgets, knickknacks, and smartphones. (Even if the phone or gadget you currently have works just fine.)

+ Post all these luxuries and materials on social media to make sure others know you checked these success items off your list. (Even if you are miserable, deep in debt, and your relationships are on the brink of disaster.)

This, my friends, is the definition of American success.

+ How did you measure up?
+ Are you "successful"?
+ Did you work hard to get these items checked off, even if it came at the expense of true joy?
+ Or, have you felt like a failure because you haven't acquired these things?

You and I were given this list subconsciously as we were sitting in those stiff grade-school desks preparing for adulthood. Through the media, movies, and the now-ubiquitous reality TV shows, the powers that be worked hard to make sure we use *their* definition of what it means to be successful instead of creating our own.

A New Reality

"Kimora! Get in here and tell me what you think about this dress!" screamed a beautiful young woman on the television. The reality show, *Kimora: House of Fab*, was blaring in the background, and I turned toward the television to see the dress this girl was being so frantic about. Kimora Simmons, a fashion model and the former wife of business mogul Russel Simmons, sauntered into the room looking mildly annoyed and responded sharply to the young girl.

I watch her. I watch them. *She's so beautiful*, I think. *Why can't my hair be as long as hers? Look at her house! My entire apartment is the size of her kitchen!*

Without even being fully aware of it, I start to feel a little down. She's gorgeous, she's a successful businesswoman, *and* she has beautiful kids! She has all the things we all want! The career, the house, the money, the cars, AND the exposure of it all. My shoulders start to droop, and I sigh. I am reminded, once again, of all the boxes on American Society's list of success that I have yet to check off. I am reminded, once again, that I don't measure up.

Have you ever felt this way after viewing a show or looking at social media? Well, it's not by mistake. Let's take a short trip into the neighborhood to find out why.

Dear Mr. Jones—Won't You Be My Neighbor?

In 1913, the phrase "keeping up with the Joneses" originated as a comic strip. In the 1950s, as the US economy became stronger with the rise of industrialism, more Americans, like ships on the tide, rose into the realms of the middle class. Jobs were stable, incomes were strong, pensions were permanent, and the amount of discretionary spending steadily increased.

Television was a calmer beast back then, barely purring out suggestions of inadequateness, and people weren't really aware of the conspicuous spending of the ultra-elite. Basically, middle-class and working-class people weren't seeing all the ways the rich were spending their wealth like we see it today. But the middle class did see something.

They saw their neighbors.

"Did you see Bob pulling up in his new 1952 Ford next door? Did you catch the new washing machine that Gladys' husband bought her for her birthday?" People were watching one another. This is what the people were seeing and saying. They noticed what their neighbors were driving, wearing, and buying. So, the original use of the phrase, "keeping up with the Joneses," is actually a neighborhood-based model of what your neighbors were consuming.

"Keeping up with the Joneses" is you wanting to stay on par with *their* consumerism, the consumerism of your physical neighbors. You had no idea, or didn't really care, what Clark Gable or Marilyn Monroe were buying or how they lived. You didn't have continuous visual access to the ultra-wealthy, like we do today. You were concerned with comparing yourself to your neighbors, one purchase at a time.

The Joneses Have Left—Enter the Kardashians

With the onset of reality television, a new comparison model quietly arose, appearing on our TVs, dancing into homes, and subsequently planting itself into our subconscious. No longer were we just concerned with Bob next door and what he got his wife for Christmas. Now, we had a different, more impossible, yardstick to measure ourselves against. This yardstick will end up taking its toll on our identities, our definition of success, and, subsequently, our country's happiness.

Remember the 1980s show that showcased the extravagant homes and luxuries of the wealthy called *Lifestyles of the Rich and Famous?* Hosted by Robin Leach and his streaky voice, that was our first peek into what it was to be rich—filthy rich. The cars, the helicopter pads, and the houses—or rather mansions—graced our screens to introduce us to a world we previously didn't really know, or care, was there.

Today, we certainly know and feel that the rich exist, because they're in our homes incessantly. It never ends. The Joneses have left—moved away. The Joneses have been replaced with the Kardashians. Waking up beautiful, enjoying exquisite huge homes, and only driving luxury cars is the message we are receiving.

Now, if you have the financial foundation to operate at this level of consumption, then that's your choice. But for most Americans, especially with stagnant wages and the rising cost of living, we are leveraging our futures and our happiness in an attempt to maintain this façade of living.

We're working hard, often at jobs we're not passionate about, to keep up with the elusive 1 percent—the untouchable 1 percent. It takes a great deal of money and energy to keep up with the Kardashians. This ends up being a costly choice in more ways than one.

Time is one of the biggest costs that usually slips by unnoticed.

Chapter Thirteen

(Inner Game)
TIME IS ON YOUR SIDE
. . . OR IS IT?

Time Is on My Side

It's 2:35 p.m. The school day is about to end. Looking at my students, I get ready to do our public service announcement (PSA). My fifth graders are about to graduate from elementary school, and I give them a few life hacks before they move on to the next phase of life—middle school.

"All right, class, I have a question for you," I started off saying, one by one their eyes turned in my direction. A hush came over the room.

"What's the worst thing you can steal from me?" I asked them.

Silence.

Thinking about how I can rephrase the question, I started again.

"If you steal my phone, I'd be upset, but could I go get another one?"

They all nodded.

"If you take my wallet, you'll probably get suspended but still, could I replace those items?"

They nodded again, wondering where I was going with this.

"But what if you took my time?" A few eyebrows went up. "What if I let you waste my time? Is that worse?" I glanced around to see if anyone was starting to see where I was leading.

"I think so, Ms. Letford, because you can't go to the store and buy more time," my youngest student, Fatima shared.

"Yes!" I exclaimed, pointing in her direction. "Exactly!"

Our Most Valuable Resource

It's interesting how we spend a significant amount of money protecting various things in our life. We have home alarm systems for our houses, LoJacks on our cars, and geometric pass codes for our phones. We are intentional on making sure these items are protected. We leave nothing to chance when it comes to our stuff. But we leave one of the most important resources out in the open for anyone to steal. What is it?

Our time!

We don't protect our time—which is arguably the most valuable *nonrenewable* resource we have.

But Genein, you ask, *how does this deal with my finances?* What does time have to do with the way I consume.

I'm glad you asked!

It is connected more than you know. When I came to this realization, it affected every dollar that left my household.

The Trade of a Lifetime

Unless you are independently wealthy—which means you are able to live off the interest of your *personally invested* resources, you are in need of acquiring money to live. Where do you get this money? You work. You work hard. After you work, the company gives you money. You are basically trading your time and expertise for money.

Have you stopped to really think about this?

If you make twenty dollars an hour, the company is not just paying you for giving them an hour. You could do that on your couch at home. They are paying for your skills and the value you put into that hour. Nevertheless, it is still an hour of your time. It is an hour of your day, month, and year.

It is an hour of *your life.*

Before you even see that money, Uncle Sam takes a chunk of it and sends it off to pay the bills of the nation. So, the first hour or two of your day goes straight to the government in the form of taxes. The rest of the day is paid to you in the form of money. This was a trade. Time and value for twenty dollars an hour. When we get what is left, we really don't see it as a trade for our time. We see it as a paycheck. Just as money.

But what if we were to see our paycheck differently? See it for the result of the transaction it really is. What if we were to see it as actual time?

When I viewed my Bank of America credit card bill (which was the catalyst to my rock-bottom moment) there was $161 going to interest payments every month. So, if I was making $20 an hour, that was over *eight hours* of my time going straight to Bank of America in the form of interest. Paying interest is like money being burned up. It is your dollars dying a slow, meaningless death. With this new way of seeing things, I saw my dollars, and therefore my time, heading to the graveyard.

This was another reason I needed to get my financial life in order. I was wasting my life by sending money to places of demise. These final resting graveyards were not building my net worth nor were they places that I supported, like my church or organizations that do good in the community. My money was dying, day by day, hour by hour. I needed for that to stop.

Do you?

For most of us, our money is a trade for our life. So, invest your *life* wisely. Make sure you are getting a return for the investment of your days. Make sure time, and your money, is on your side.

Chapter Fourteen

(Inner Game)
CARS: THE SUBTLE
FORCE ON OUR
FINANCIAL FREEDOM

The Financial Drain on the Middle Class

Where is one of the worst places to spend our money and our time? Yep, you probably guessed it by the title of this chapter.

Cars.

Many of us have them, and unless you live in a city that has an efficient public transportation system, many of us need them. I live in Los Angeles, so traveling in a car is more of a necessity than if I lived in Boston or New York City. Nevertheless, what's the true cost to our financial foundation of that car we own?

Looking at my budget while we were paying off debt, I realized our transportation budget was 20 percent of our take-home income. Our car payment was $350, our car insurance was $120, and top that off with gas, we were paying almost $600 a month for transportation—$600 a month!

This was more than we were saving, investing, or giving. This total amount was going straight to our transportation.

This made me stop and reflect on that line item of our budget. What is the actual return on investment of a car? True, it gets me to work and back so I can make money. But that is all it does!

It transports my body from home to work, to church and back home. It doesn't make me any smarter, any healthier, any kinder, or more spiritual. There's no other external or internal benefit. It moves my mind and my body from one location to another.

That's it.

So, here I am giving 20 percent of my take-home income to a budget item that has no high return on investment. No additional elements to my life. And if you factor in the time concept I just mentioned, at twenty dollars an hour, I was giving *thirty hours of my life* per month to transportation! With that sober thought, we decided to lower that line item as much as possible. The return on investment on a vehicle was much too low.

In my opinion, cars are one of the *worst investments* in which to spend our money. Yet for many American families, transportation is the highest line item, right after housing. The ubiquitous car payment—nearly everyone has one. It is normal to not only have a car but to own one that is significantly above our financial capabilities. Why am I discussing cars in the value section of this book? This has everything to do with our perceived value and how we see ourselves. We have been trained to communicate our value through our vehicles. Trained? Yes, trained.

 Here are some red flags to warn us about our relationship with our cars.

+ If the value of your car is higher than your yearly income—that's a red flag.
+ If the value of your car is higher than your savings/investment accounts—that's a red flag.

♦ If your monthly car payment is higher than what you are saving/ investing per month— that's a red flag.

♦ If you're unwilling to sell your expensive car to reach your financial freedom goals—that's a red flag.

These red flags aren't meant to make us feel bad or condemn us. These red flags are meant to cause us to stop and think, *Hmmm, will I like where the outcome of this choice is taking me in twenty-five years?* If most of your money is going into a car, where is it truly going?

The junkyard.

Yep, that's right. All your car payments are, in essence, heading straight into the junkyard, because that is where your beloved car is going to end up—eventually. Whether it's next week due to a car accident (hopefully this doesn't happen) or it's in twenty years due to normal wear and tear (this will happen to all cars), all your money and your investment of life is going straight to the junkyard. Ouch!

Do you know people who make $30,000 a year but drive $60,000 cars? They struggle to make payments on their Mercedes, BMWs, and Jaguars? Why is this? Well, it's designed this way and, once again, it all comes back to the psychology of consumerism. It's what we value and how we want people to perceive our success, or rather our idea of success.

The Jedi Mind Trick of Car Dealers

Car dealerships can be dangerous places for our financial wealth. Some car salespeople are even more dangerous. They know how the value systems of most Americans are rooted in appearance and superficial success. They have spent time learning the Jedi mind tricks to get your purchases to reflect this. I believe more money is lost on the car showroom floor than anywhere else, including the stock market.

I will detail this psychology of consumerism in section seven, but I will mention here that car salespeople know how Americans attach their identities to their cars. Since the first Ford rolled off the assembly line in the early 1900s, the prestige of owning a vehicle, and now a nice luxury vehicle, spoke to what type of person you were and the respect you sought. Like my 1999 Nissan story at the LAX airport, people automatically judge your success by the quality of your vehicle. Be honest. You have done this. I know I have.

And yet, it makes no sense!

The two have absolutely nothing in common. Your worth as a person is in no way reflective of the worth of your vehicle. I know this. You know this. But most Americans, especially on the West Coast, believe the best way to communicate their value, worth, and success is connected to what they drive. The funny thing is, in the 1800s, everyone had horses and only the wealthy owned cars. Now, everyone has a car and those who own horses are wealthy. Isn't life interesting?

These Aren't the Prices You're Looking For

The Jedi mind trick in *Star Wars* was a perfect example of misdirection. It's clever how car dealers use this same tactic. They know it's not about the car or even the total price, it's about what you focus on. You and I can have the same stats (credit score, income, down payment, etc.) and buy the same exact car. But depending on what we're focusing on, we will pay completely different amounts, sometimes in the range of a $5,000 difference for *the same exact car.*

"So what type of payment are you looking to have?" the dealer asked me, as I slid into the driver's seat of the KIA Optima. It's 2014 and, even though we're still paying off debt, I am doing my research on the new car I'll need to get once my debt is paid off.

"I'm not worried about the monthly payment," I tell him, glancing at him in the rearview mirror. My husband is in the passenger seat, occupied with all the buttons near the dashboard. "I'm focused on the total price of the car."

This is how they get you.

"Please focus on the monthly payment instead of focusing on the entire price of the car," they say in their Jedi voice, while waving their fingers in front of your eyes. They understand that if they lower the payment for you, to an amount you can afford monthly, it will allow you to get into a more expensive car. What they don't want you to focus on is the extended terms. What they want you to ignore is the extra time you're paying interest— free money that goes straight to them. What they don't want you to see is all the dollars you traded your time for, going straight to the junkyard.

Speaking Your Language

Salespeople are experts at finding your selling points—finding out what moves you—finding out what you value. What is important to you might not be important to me. It is to their benefit to listen to you to discover what will cause you to buy.

+ Are you a parent?
+ Do you care about safety?
+ Do you care about looking good?
+ Do you like finessing?
+ Are you a tree hugger and desire to be as green as possible?
+ Are you a penny pincher and want the best fuel economy?
+ Do you have low funds but want a nice ride?
+ Are you a desperate buyer who has no car and needs one right away?

Once the salespeople establish those motivation points, then they move the focus from those details to the part of you that gets you to act— your feelings and emotions.

+ How does this car make you feel?
  - Like a rock star?
  - Like a responsible parent?
  - Like a protector of the environment?

+ Where are your value points?
+ How can we translate them into your dream car?

These are the mind tricks they play, and boy are they successful. The number of working-class and middle-class people who are driving cars they cannot afford because of high or incessant car payments is staggering. In addition to stagnant wages and other economic factors, I think the ubiquitous car payment is another significant factor to the slow decline of the middle class.

This is why it is important to know your value with or without the car. It's also important to know your numbers before you even step foot on a car lot. Try to save up cash for a used, *reliable* car. If you cannot save up to pay cash for the car and you have to put it on payments, try not to go over a three-year term. Suze Orman, the financial guru, says if you can't pay off a car in three years or less, *it's too much car.* Now dealerships and banks have sixty-month terms and leases for a car. *Sixty months!* That is five years of paying interest on an item that will one day be rusting in a junkyard. Be aware of that true cost of this decision on your life.

If you don't understand your value and your numbers, the trained salespeople will throw logic out the window and sell you on your emotions. This is the easiest way to overpay for a vehicle that has such low return on your investment.

We Americans love our cars! That's ok! Let's just make sure our other financial goals are met before we make such a costly investment.

Lucifer's Leasing Plan

"Two thousand dollars!" I heard her gasp, as she yelled that number. Renewing my license at the AAA counter, I look to my left at the astonished woman giving an exasperated glare at the AAA representative.

"But the purchase price is only $20,000! Where did this extra $2,000 come from?" she exclaimed.

"Ma'am," the AAA rep responded in a calm voice, "I know you're buying out your Lexus lease, but you know you have to pay tax on the car, right?" The representative looked at her and then down at the paperwork, almost in disbelief that the customer was unaware of this process.

"But, but," she stammered, "I took out a second loan on my house for this exact amount. I don't have the $2,000." She looked defeated.

I turned my head away to look down at my registration renewal I had to sign, pretending I wasn't listening. But I was. *Wow,* I thought, *it has come down to this. We really do love our cars.*

I have been in many debates about leasing and only one position has gotten my support. To me, leasing vehicles is the same as throwing money out the window, money that we know was a trade for our time. Money that could be used to build wealth for our families and our futures.

In case you're unsure how leasing works, here's a rundown. First and foremost, it is a system in place to make sure the car dealership doesn't lose the cost of a depreciating vehicle. Leasing protects them, not you. The way leasing works is different from buying a car outright with cash or purchasing the car and putting it on a fixed monthly payment for an agreed term because at the end of the term, you own the car outright.

With leasing you're basically "renting" the car for a certain amount of money for an agreed length of time. During your lease term, you can only drive it a certain number of miles. If you go over that number, you will pay a penalty per mile. Once the lease term ends, you have a few options; you can buy the car from the dealer, return the car, get a lease on a new car, or walk away with nothing.

The reason I think this is a bad financial practice is that you will always have a car payment and, unless you purchase the car after the lease, like the woman at AAA was trying to do, you will never end up owning the car. If your lease payment was $350 for thirty-six months, you just handed over $12,600, then you have to *give the car back* after the lease is completed. For people who are focused on building wealth, they know this is not the way to do it.

Now, the best argument I heard in favor of leasing is a from a fellow teacher in Boston.

"Genein, I know you do not like leasing but here in New England, I don't want to be stuck in four feet of snow with a twelve-year-old car that won't start," he argued.

I nodded. "Ok, I understand where you're coming from. But still, that's a lot of money you're just giving to the bank for barely anything in return."

"I know, I know. But honestly, I like having a new car every three years. It brings me joy," he added.

I like that. He's self-aware and honest. Hopefully, he calculated the true cost of owning that leased vehicle. Will this joy be there when he realizes he's underfunded for his retirement or still paying off student loans at fifty? I pray he took the time to figure out the *true cost* of that perpetual payment. (We'll discuss that next.)

Leasing does have its upside. In addition to having a new ride every three to five years, you get to experience new technology more often than someone who owns their car for ten or more years. I drove my 1999 Sentra from the year 2000 to the end of 2017. When I was ready to buy my used 2015 KIA, my friend asked what type of "bells and whistles" I was excited to get in my new ride.

Bells and whistles?

Geez, if it had a working CD player, I was a happy camper! Oh, and Bluetooth. I really wanted Bluetooth. Today, those features come standard in vehicles but back then, Bluetooth was an extra. If you upgrade your lease every three years, you get to be on the cutting edge of car technology. Just don't forget, there is a cost to every choice—even the bells-and-whistle choices!

Here's how to calculate that critical cost.

Chapter Fifteen

(Inner Game)
THE COST OF YOUR
LOST OPPORTUNITIES

If you remember in chapter one, we talked about making a decision. The fact that you are this far into the book, I'm hoping you made that decision by now. But let me tell you one thing about decisions.

Decisions aren't free.

They come at a cost. In economics, they call this concept *opportunity cost*. For example, if you choose between having a piece of pie or a cookie, you lose out on experiencing one of those choices. If you choose the cookie, you lose out on enjoying the pie. Choose the pie? Then no cookie for you! The lost experience is the cost of your choice.

The problem arises in finances because we do not fully recognize or understand the opportunity cost of our financial choices. This is mostly because of slick marketing and ignorance of financial literacy. When it comes to opportunity cost, only *you* can truly calculate whether the opportunity cost is worth it.

For instance, this next story shows the high price of not factoring the cost of our decisions. I ran into a friend at church. He's an amazing twenty-eight-year-old young man with a strong work ethic. He has such a great heart for people, and you can see his compassion for others as he dances and while he serves others. His smile is infectious.

He drove up one Wednesday in a beautiful white BMW, pumping the music and looking fly. It was sleek. It was nice. He got himself a nice whip, and he knew it. I lingered in the parking lot a bit to wait for him to get out of his car, because I wanted to do some soft research.

"Hey, Emmanuel! I'm liking this ride you're rolling up in!"

He flashed that bright infectious smile.

"Is it new?" I asked.

"Nope," he responded, shaking his head, "I just got it off a lease but now I'm buying it."

I sighed a happy sigh because deep down, I loathe car leases.

"Well, I'm glad you're *buying* the car!" I happily retorted. "If I might ask," I paused, "how much was the total lease?" I lightened my voice so he wouldn't feel like I was prying.

"Well, I paid them $14,000 for a three-year lease," he said matter-of-factly. My eyebrows went up. I nodded.

"Ok," I said, "And for the purchase? What did that factor out to be?"

"The terms were good—I think." His confidence wavered a bit, and he started to sound unsure. "I'm paying about $470 for sixty months," he answered me. I was appreciative he was sharing this information with me, because people get secretive when it comes to talking about their financial numbers, especially income or debt.

"Well, thank you for the info. I'm doing some soft research for my book and have one other question for you." My eyes turned toward his car and then returned to meet his.

"The amount that you are paying into your car—do you have that same amount in your savings or retirement accounts?"

Silence.

His eyes shifted upward and to the right, and he began to chuckle, "No, not quite."

"Ok. That's cool," I reassured him. "Do you have *anything* in your savings or retirement?" I searched his face, hopeful he would say that he had at least a couple of dollars in his savings.

"Weeelllll," he dragged that word out like he was about to break out singing a Negro spiritual.

"Nothing?" I chimed in, cutting off his high-pitched note.

He shook his head.

"Ok, no worries," I smiled slowly, trying not to let the panic creep into my voice. "Well, if you want more information about setting those up, just let me know. I'm here."

He nodded enthusiastically and sauntered off to rehearsal.

The following week, I saw him in church, and he came straight for me.

"Genein," he started, "I've been thinking about what you were asking me, and I realized I don't know anything about retirement accounts. I would love to talk to you more about that."

"I totally get it! I didn't know about them either when I was your age," I assured him. "But what breaks my heart is that you didn't know what you were trading in with that decision. Most people don't. Do you know how to factor your opportunity cost?"

"My what?" he had a confused look on his face.

"Opportunity cost," I repeated slower. "Basically, it's what you're giving up in place of choosing the car. Watch this." I brought out my phone. "How much did you pay for the lease?"

"Fourteen thousand dollars," he replied, "and the payments are $470 for sixty months to buy the car."

"Ok, so that's . . ." I punched away at my trusty calculator, "$28,200 to buy the car plus $14,000 for the lease, right?"

He nodded.

I pressed the total button and looked at the sum of those numbers. "So, in five years, you will have handed BMW a grand total of $42,200 of your hard-earned money and," I continued slowly for emphasis, "there is *nothing* in your own savings account."

His eyes got big. I don't think he ever added up the total cost of the car. I could be wrong.

"But that's not even the opportunity cost I'm talking about," I continued. "Let's say, instead of leasing the BMW, you saved up for a decent used car and decided to drive that around for a while. You put that BMW money into an investment account instead. That account earns a modest 8 percent—some say it could earn 10 to 12 percent—but we're going to be conservative and stick with 8 percent off the bat. Let's just say . . ."

I pulled up the investment calculator and punched in the numbers.

"Let's just say for those five years, beginning at twenty-eight years old, you were investing that money and then you stopped at age thirty-three." I paused and glanced at him to make sure I wasn't going too fast. "How much do you think you would have in your account when you were ready to retire at sixty-seven years old?"

"I dunno," his shoulders shrugged. "Maybe $50,000?

I looked at my phone. I glanced up at him, smiled and showed him the number.

"It's $577,723!" I slowly said, like I was announcing a grand prize on *The Price Is Right* TV show. "And this is at an 8 percent return. If the market averages 10 percent, you would have had over one million dollars sitting in your account."

He looked stunned.

"And almost two million dollars if the market averaged 12 percent!" I kept my mouth closed and let that number sink in.

He took a slow deep sigh, "Wow."

"All from only eight years of investing your BMW money into an investment account. But you don't see that money because you traded that one million dollars for a car," I shrugged and continued, "which will probably be rusting in a junkyard by the time you're sixty-seven."

I waited for a response. He still was silent, so I continued.

"That, my friend, is opportunity cost. Now there's no guilt. No condemnation here. There's no right or wrong choice," I showed him the phone one last time. "Just be aware of the *cost* of your choice." I put my hand on his shoulder for reassurance. "Because there's always a cost."

Talking to him and showing him that all our decisions have costs, whether we are aware of them or not, made him go back and analyze all his other financial decisions. He's now fired up to get himself on a better financial track.

Now, I'm not telling him to never buy a luxury car. I'm not saying he should never have nice things. I'm showing him that the money he's working so hard for is going into a depreciating object when instead it could be appreciating or growing. I'm advising him to choose to invest while he's young, so he can buy those nice things when he's standing on a more stable financial foundation, even though he might be a little older. It's worth the wait. Trust me. We all should factor in the opportunity cost and decide, for ourselves, if we are ok with it. In the end, it's up to us and it depends on our values and goals.

For instance, I bought a 2015 KIA for $15,000 at the end of 2017. I could have purchased an older car for $5,000 and invested the $10,000. At an 8 percent return, when I am sixty-seven years old, that $10,000 would have been $93,172. But I didn't do that. I bought the car for $15,000. I had to be ok with that decision of paying the opportunity cost of not investing that money. I felt content about my decision, because I spent the past seven years paying off debt, investing and saving up cash for the car. This was an opportunity cost I was willing to forgo to drive my fabulous KIA Optima! I adore that car!

Go for Your Dream Car the Right Way

Once again, it might sound like I'm beating up on luxury car ownership and leasing. I'm not. I want everyone to print out their dream luxury car and post it on their vision board. You should have fun with what you drive. Why not? This is America after all. We love our cars!

The main thing is to keep it in perspective. If you logically weigh the benefits and costs of these big decisions, it will pay off in the long run. Like

Emmanuel, time is on your side if you understand these concepts earlier in life. If I run into one more family that has no savings, no college plan for the kids, no life insurance, and nothing in retirement for the parents, yet they are joy riding in a $60,000 leased or financed car, I'm going to scream. These cars are financially killing the working-class and middle-class' ability to build wealth. It's a price we *all have to pay* in the long run if it continues.

> *"Being prepared and awaiting the unprepared is victory."*
>
> —Sun Tsu

Buying-a-Used-Car Hacks

If you are looking to build wealth and make smarter financial decisions, one of them should be purchasing a used car instead of a new car. New cars lose 20 percent of their value in their first year and approximately 10 percent of their value every year after that. If you buy used, you won't get hit with that huge depreciation like new car owners do. Here are my tips with buying used cars with wisdom.

Look for Low Mileage

In 2018, I was researching 2015 KIA Optima with a price point of $15,000. I found one that had 53,000 miles and one that had 23,000 miles. With everything else the same, which one was the better deal?

Research before Entering into a Negotiation

The one with the most information has an advantage. Research the range of prices people have paid for that very same car. Know the cost of operating the car (depreciation cost, gas and maintenance expenses, etc.). Visit the websites or phone apps of Edmunds, True Car Value or Kelly Blue Book for this critical information.

CarMax Versus Car Lots

CarMax is a "no haggle" used car business where the price on the car is the price you pay. This is a benefit because you can compare it to the purchased prices found in your research. Carmax salepeople don't work on commission, so there's lower chance of them 'taking you to the bank' and jacking up the price on the car to jack up their commission. Nevertheless, there is no negotiating so if you are an excellent negotiator or you want a brand-new car, a new car lot may be a better option.

Check the Vehicle Identification Number (VIN)

Let's face it, used cars come with baggage. They have a history and it's your job to find out what that is. If you're buying a used car, be sure to check that the car hasn't been in any huge accidents, was totaled and refurbished or was submerged in water. Some cars have been recalled or have other huge mechanical issues. This is not information you want to be surprised with after you purchase the car. Go to www.vehiclehistory.com and input the VIN of the desired car to discover any past information that could affect your decision.

Know the Warranty and Tax Details

Cars can be purchased anywhere, and city tax rates change depending where you are. I purchased my car in a city that had 9 percent tax rate. However, had I driven 20 miles to a city that had a 6 percent tax rate, I could have saved $400! CarMax transfers cars from one lot to another depending where you are (usually for free), so using that company would have been a strategic move.

Be aware of buying warranties you don't need. Some warranties have large loopholes and exclusions in the fine print. Ask to take the warranty home and review it closely before you purchase it. Be aware if the car you are buying already has a decent warranty. If you finance the purchase with a bank or credit union, they may have better option for extended warranties. Do your research.

Remember, your car is only meant to get you from point A to point B safely. It is not who you are as a person. Purchase a reliable car if you need one and get back to fulfilling your destiny!

Chapter Sixteen

(Inner Game)
CREATING A WINNING
VALUE GAME

Creating a winning value position is possible if you are proactive in certain areas. Here are some tips to win at the constant battle on having a healthy mindset of your value and its relationship to your financial health.

Metacognition—Think about What You Think About

One way to triumph in this area of knowing and implementing our values is to employ metacognition. That's just a fancy way to say start thinking about your thinking. Be aware of your thinking when you are planning on making a purchase or shopping. Be aware of how advertisements cause you to feel certain emotions about yourself and others. I dive deep into this strategy in chapter twenty-five, but it's worth mentioning here in the chapter about understanding your true value.

When we don't see ourselves as valuable, it's easy to attempt to fill our lives with items that will make us feel worthier of people's love and respect.

We add these material things to our lives, believing we are adding more reasons for validation—even if we can't afford these materials outright.

Now that you have read this chapter, you won't let that fool you. You'll be aware of your thinking and recalibrate any erroneous beliefs you might have when it comes to your stuff and its effect on your worth.

You are worthy! You are loved! You are you!

Reevaluating Success

> *"Man [surprised me most about humanity].*
> *Because he sacrifices his health in order to make*
> *money. Then he sacrifices money to recuperate his*
> *health. And then he is so anxious about the future*
> *that he does not enjoy the present; the result being*
> *that he does not live in the present or the future;*
> *he lives as if he is never going to die, and then dies*
> *having never really lived."*
>
> —Dalai Lama

We spend the first half of our lives learning. We acquire skills, memorize formulas, and, if we're lucky, we get to develop creative skills in preparation to work and hopefully contribute. We're then catapulted into the workforce for twenty-five or thirty years, earning a living to provide for our families and ourselves. We blindly go through our checklist of life goals—get the degree, get the car, get the spouse, get the house, get the better car, get the bigger house, and, for some, a prettier younger spouse. We've been conditioned to set our goals on *which item do we upgrade next?*

Mellody Hobson, president of Ariel Investments, puts it best, "When you are always wanting more money, you find out that it just equates to another suit or an additional room on the house. After a while, it doesn't do it for you anymore."

When the sun is setting on our time here and we breathe our last breath, we realize what life was really all about. We realize that the things we worked so hard to be able to buy, to show others and ourselves that we "made it"—the cars, the huge houses, the designer shoes, the expensive knickknacks that are now collecting dust somewhere in the attic—weren't worth the time we traded to afford them.

Lying there, we realize the things in life that have the most value, the things in life we should have focused on building and cherishing, had no price tag at all. The precious things in life having the highest value items cost us nothing: our relationships, our friendships, our connection to our creator, our ability to give a helping hand to others. Those are the areas worth investing in and protecting.

But you need to decide what has the most value in *your* life. No one can make that list for you.

So, as you review your life and your definition of success, be clear about what is important to you. Maybe it is a nice car, maybe it's not. Maybe it's being able to travel with your children, maybe it's not. Your list is a dynamic document and will evolve as time passes, because you evolved due to new experiences and relationships. Whatever goes on your list, be clear about the cost of your decisions and which direction those choices will take you, because they are taking you somewhere.

Know that you are valuable, no matter what items you own or do not own. If people only want to be around you because of what you own, then you should immediately reevaluate those relationships. Understand that you can live a life free of financial stress. You can create ways of stewarding your money with wisdom. You can choose to purchase luxury items, if you wish, knowing you have already set up a stable financial and emotional foundation for you and your family.

Take time and reflect on what success looks like to you in the areas of finance, family, health, and spiritual and physical development. This, my friends, is time well spent.

My Definition of Success

"*Success is the peace of mind attained only through self-satisfaction in knowing you made the effort to do the best of which you are capable.*"

—JOHN WOODEN

Section Four Summary

1. Create your own definition of success, or society will give you an unattainable superficial one.

2. Time is your most valuable resource, so be mindful what you invest it in.

3. Cars depreciate and are the biggest drains of wealth for the middle and working class.

4. Learn how to calculate the opportunity cost of your financial decisions.

5. Truly believe you are valuable, no matter what material possessions you own or do not own.

Section Five
DITCHING THE DEBT

Chapter Seventeen
(Outer Game)
THE DEBT FREEZE: SNOWBALL VS. AVALANCHE

"Without strategy, execution is aimless. Without execution, strategy is useless."

—MORRIS CHANG

Pick Your Weapon

Now that you defined success for yourself, it's time to get rid of the items that are pulling you away from it, like your bad debt. Earlier, you made a decision to get rid of your debt, but now you need a plan. The debt will not disappear by itself. There needs to be an action plan. Those who have a bias for action are the ones who get things done, even if they make a mistake or two along the way. We must act. We must be on the offensive. We must have a game plan. We must attack.

But we must *attack* with a *strategy*.

When it comes to acting toward your debt, there are three effective methods that you can choose from: the snowball method, the avalanche method, or a mixture of both. Both methods focus on attacking one debt account at a time (while making minimum payments on your other accounts). The differing factor is how you order the debts you're tackling. The snowball method has you order them by total account balance. The avalanche method has you order them by interest rate. The avalanche method is mathematically more efficient, but the snowball method is psychologically more motivating.

You'll need the motivation.

Once you become savvy with how credit cards, loans, and financing works, you'll feel more comfortable going through the methods and modifying them where you see fit. Here are the two methods in greater detail and how Shayne and I actually used both of them to pay off our $100,000 debt.

This is our initial debt table.

Table A

Name	Total Balance Amount	Minimum Payment	APR
Bank of America (BofA)	$8,220	$271	27%
Capital One—Shayne	$2,115	$50	27%
Capital One—Genein	$3,776	$50	18%
Dell	$962	$25	25%
Target	$2,146	$75	24%
Express	$98	$25	24%
Toyota Car Loan	$13,976	$333	7.6%
Student Loan—Shayne	$3,533	$99	3.2%
Student Loan—Genein	$56,509	$379	3.3%
Totals	**$91,335**	**$1,307**	

Snowball Fights

We've all seen it. The little snowball at the top of the hill. You push it down the hill, and it gains speed. Gathering snow, it gets bigger and bigger and bigger, demolishing anything that stands in its path. Well, that's the force you are about to put against your debt. Even though the snowball method has been made famous by Dave Ramsey, he didn't invent it. Someone's grandma did. It's been around for ages. Nevertheless, I'm glad Dave made it famous, or I would have never discovered it as a strategy to use against my debilitating debt.

If you're just making minimum payments on all your debt, you will be in bondage for a long time. Credit cards and loans are set up that way—to keep you in debt for life. So, why not pay a little bit above the minimum payments on all your accounts at the same time? Now, you're diffusing your power. It's like flicking a little pellet against your debt instead of bringing in the big guns. Money is power, and if your power is spread all over the place, there's no real impact. It's diffused. It's weak.

Like a laser, when you focus your power onto one particular spot. Kaboom!

That is what the snowball and avalanche methods do. They both help you zero in your monetary power laser to one particular debt.

Remember, clarity brings focus, and focus moves you forward.

The Snowball Method

For the snowball method, place your debts in order from smallest balance to largest balance. Ignore the interest rate or the amount of the minimum payment. Once your debts are in order, look at the smallest debt. Glare at it. It's going down! This is the first debt you will be focusing on with your extra payment power. Any extra money you have after you have modified your budget and taken out all the unnecessary expenses, go hurling at this debt. Any money you drummed up from garage sales or selling your diamond earrings an old boyfriend gave you or that extra side job you worked goes here.

Table B—Snowball—Balance from Lowest to Highest

Name	Total Balance Amount	Minimum Payment	Payment Sent
Express	$98	$25	$98
Dell	$962	$25	$25
Capital One—Shayne	$2,115	$50	$50
Target	$2,146	$75	$75
Student Loan—Shayne	$3,533	$99	$99
Capital One—Genein	$3,776	$50	$50
BofA	$8,220	$271	$271
Toyota Car Loan	$13,976	$333	$333
Student Loan—Genein	$56,509	$379	$379

In my example, I started tutoring (and I did have old diamond earrings that needed to go) and was able to bring in an extra $100 a month in addition to paying all my expenses and minimum payments. So, the first bill I attacked was my Express credit card with a payment of $98. The minimum payment was $25 but with the extra $100 I added to my snowball, I paid the entire debt off as my first step. That was easy.

Now, in the meantime, you are still paying the minimum payments on all your other accounts and your other expenses. This method is assuming that you have enough income to cover your other expenses and pay the minimum payment on your other debts. You already called your creditors to get the current balance and information. You already asked for a lower interest rate or to be put in a payoff program, if applicable. You did the work. Now it's time to attack that smallest debt and attack it hard.

Once you have paid off that smallest debt, celebrate. Do a dance. Go buy some frozen yogurt! Celebrate the momentum you'll be gaining as you head to your second smallest debt. Now, with that debt, you are continuing to pay the minimum payment *plus* the payment you were sending to the first debt.

The second smallest bill was our Dell account with a balance of $962 at that time. The original minimum payment was $25 but now with the Express card paid and the extra $100 added to my snowball, I can send in a payment of $150 per month. Bullseye! Pay that debt off completely in a few months and do a cartwheel in your living room.

Table C

Name	Total Balance Amount	Minimum Payment	Payment Sent
Express	$0	$0	$0
Dell	$962	$25	*$150*
Capital One—Shayne	$2,115	$50	$50
Target	$2,146	$75	$75
Student Loan—Shayne	$3,533	$99	$99
Capital One—Genein	$3,776	$50	$50
BofA	$8,220	$271	$271
Toyota Car Loan	$13,976	$333	$333
Student Loan—Genein	$56,509	$379	$379

Now onto the third smallest debt. This debt not only has the minimum payment going toward it but also the payments you were paying on the first two cards. Do you see why it's called the snowball method? The snowball is getting bigger and more powerful, and those debts are going down. I couldn't wait for payday, just so I could pay off the debt. My heart would flutter when I would press "send" to pay down a bill.

If you are solely doing the snowball method, you could continue this process until all your debts are paid off but your mortgage. Once that is done, you really celebrate! This method works best if you need a motivational push.

Table D

Name	Total Balance Amount	Minimum Payment	Payment Sent
Express	$0	$0	
Dell	$0	$0	
Capital One—Shayne	$2,115	$50	$200
Target	$2,146	$75	$75
Student Loan—Shayne	$3,533	$99	$99
Capital One—Genein	$3,776	$50	$50
BofA	$8,220	$271	$271
Toyota Car Loan	$13,976	$333	$333
Student Loan—Genein	$56,509	$379	$379

Avalanche Method

I know several people who would cringe at the snowball method. Why? Because it doesn't take into account the interest rate. The higher the interest rate, the more money the bank is adding to your principal amount—the total amount of what you owe. Realistically, with the snowball method, you could be paying off a low interest loan while a high interest debt is sitting in the number four position steadily racking up massive finance charges.

With the avalanche method, you don't look at the balance but the interest rate instead. This way, you are effectively lowering the amount of interest you are paying in the long run. The drawback is that it might take you a while to get to that first win. It might take you a year or more, depending on the size of your first debt and cash flow, to be able to get that froyo for that initial payoff celebration.

Slow and steady wins the race but you might lose steam and give up before you get anywhere near the first finish line. With my avalanche method, I wouldn't be able to celebrate until the $8,220 balance for the BofA bill was paid. That would have been a while before I treated myself to some froyo!

Genein's Example of the Avalanche Method

Name	Total Balance Amount	Minimum Payment	APR
BofA	$8,220	$271	27%
Capital One—Shayne	$2,115	$50	27%
Dell	$962	$25	25%
Target	$2,146	$75	24%
Express	$98	$25	24%
Capital One—Genein	$3,776	$50	18%
Toyota Car Loan	$13,976	$333	7%
Student Loan—Genein	$56,509	$379	3%
Student Loan—Shayne	$3,533	$99	2%
Totals	**$91,335**	**$1,307**	

Peas and Carrots

I like peas. I like carrots. But when you put them both together, magic happens. I don't know what it is, but they're delicious! This is how I approached my debt payoff methods—combining the best of the snowball and avalanche methods.

First, I identified my debilitating debt. This is the Al Capone of debt. This is the debt that is basically trying to beat you down by kicking you in the shins, and then it knees you in the stomach. Ouch! It needs to go, and it needs to go fast. This debt carries an interest rate over 18 percent and usually ranges in the 25–30 percent zone. Financial murder. It is the quicksand for your wealth-building income. All our credit cards were in this category. We felt like we were actually in quicksand.

 Let's look at my numbers in the pure snowball order.

Table F

Name	Total Balance Amount	Minimum Payment	APR
Express	$98	$25	24%
Dell	$962	$25	25%
Capital One—Shayne	$2,115	$50	27%
Target	$2,146	$75	24%
Student Loan—Shayne	$3,533	$99	3.2%
Capital One—Genein	$3,776	$50	18%
BofA	$8,220	$271	27%
Toyota Car Loan	$13,976	$333	7.6%
Student Loan—Genein	$56,509	$379	3.3%

This would be the order if I was doing the pure snowball method. All my accounts are current, and no accounts were in threat of being charged-off. Off the bat, one issue was Shayne's student loan. It was smack in the middle of the list but only has an interest rate of 3.2 percent. It is ahead of the crushing BofA credit card, which was burning us at 27 percent on a balance of $8,220. Every time I see a Bank of America building, I have to stop myself from writing my name on a few bricks. I felt like I helped them build those buildings with my credit card interest!

So, I contemplated moving Shayne's student loan after the BofA credit card. But before I did, I made a strategic move that ended up working out in our favor.

Communicate

I know I mentioned this earlier, but it bears repeating—communicating with your creditors is key. Remember when I called Bank of America and said that we were struggling to pay this credit card due to the high interest rate and high payment? To accommodate us, and not have the card charge-off the balance, we were informed about a credit assist program that helps borrowers get a handle on their debts. The program lowers the interest rate significantly and lowers the monthly payment.

With the BofA credit card in the credit assist program, we now had an interest rate of 4 percent and a monthly payment of $120. Those numbers made us readjust our snowball list.

Table G

Name	Total Balance Amount	Minimum Payment	APR
Express	$98	$25	24%
Dell	$962	$25	25%
Capital One—Shayne	$2,115	$50	27%
Target	$2,146	$75	24%
Student Loan—Shayne	$3,533	$99	3.2%
Capital One—Genein	$3,776	$50	18%
BofA	$8,220	$120	4%
Toyota Car Loan	$13,976	$333	7.6%
Student Loan—Genein	$56,509	$379	3.3%

Continuing with our modifications, we analyzed the interest rates. Even though Shayne's student loans were less that my Capital One card, we switched those two credit cards because the balances were close but the interest rate on the Capital One card was drastically higher.

Snowball List with Cap/Student Loan Switched

Name	Total Balance Amount	Minimum Payment	APR
Express	$98	$25	24%
Dell	$962	$25	25%
Capital One—Shayne	$2,115	$50	27%
Target	$2,146	$75	24%
Capital One—Genein	$3,776	$50	18%
Student Loan—Shayne	$3,533	$99	3.2%
BofA	$8,220	$120	4%
Toyota Car Loan	$13,976	$333	7.6%
Student Loan—Genein	$56,509	$379	3.3%

Don't be so rigid, that you're unwilling to modify the order if the numbers change. It is a living document. Do what works for your situation. Be flexible but stay focused. You'll devour this debt one bite at a time.

Chapter Eighteen

(Outer Game)
CHUNKING
THE DEBT

Eating Elephants: One Bite at a Time

As I became better with handling our debt, I started to teach my other family members these strategies to get them on the road to financial freedom. My younger sister, Genette, got on the train quick! But when she added up all her debt from her and her husband's student loans, it was almost a quarter of a million dollars!

"Genein," she said to me, shaking her head, "we could have bought a house!"

JUST GETTING STARTED | **ALMOST THERE!** | **GOAL!!!**

When she listed her debt using the snowball method and placed it on her goal thermometer, she realized she had an issue. "Even if I pay off a credit card with a significant amount, I still can't color in any progress because the total debt is so large!" Yep—$3,000 wouldn't even move the needle on a total debt of $250,000! Keeping her thermometer with those large numbers didn't help with motivation either.

So, what did we do?

We chunked it.

We separated her debt into phases and placed only phase one on her thermometer. Her entire debt was the size of an elephant but right now, we're only focusing on the left toe. She can eat this elephant but only one bite at a time. I took this concept to my own debt payoff journey. Here's how I chunked my debt into four phases.

Table H

Name	Total Balance Amount	Minimum Payment	APR
PHASE ONE			
Express	$98	$25	24%
Dell	$962	$25	25%
Capital One—Shayne	$2,115	$50	27%
PHASE TWO	**CELEBRATE!**		
Target	$2,146	$75	24%
Capital One—Genein	$3,776	$50	18%
Student Loan—Shayne	$3,533	$99	3.2%
PHASE THREE	**CELEBRATE!**		
BofA	$8,220	$120	4%
Toyota Car Loan	$13,976	$333	7.6%
PHASE FOUR	**CELEBRATE!**		
Student Loan—Genein	$56,509	$379	3.3%
	CELEBRATE!	**WE'RE DEBT FREE!**	

Celebrate Good Times, Come On!

To complete phase one, we had to pay off $3,175. That's a doable goal and worth celebrating after completion. Celebration is so important. The brain loves rewards and turns on its extra tools, like the reticular activating system (RAS) I mentioned earlier, to assist you to achieve those rewards. When you remove unnecessary but enjoyable activities and treats from your budget, don't forget about them. Put them in the rewards category for completing your phases. It's a win-win!

Modifications for the Mind

Looking at each of my phases, you'll see the total amounts are getting bigger. Phase one has a total debt of $3,175, but phase three has a total debt of $22,196. Seems like a huge jump from the first phase, huh? Don't forget, by the time you get to phase two, your snowball of a payment has become more powerful and is much bigger than in phase one. But also don't forget, this is your journey, and if you need to chunk your phases into smaller sections, that's fine.

For instance, our phase four started at $56,509 when we began. By the time we got to that phase, the debt was $40,092 (due to paying the minimum payment during the previous phases and getting some debt cancelled through a teacher debt-forgiveness program). We decided to cut that amount into two subphases. Phase four-A and phase four-B, with each phase having a debt of $20,000. After we completed Phase four-A, we celebrated big time. A weekend trip to San Diego (in budget hotels though!) was the perfect end punctuation to that phase.

SMART Goals

We already reviewed setting up goals, but this is a great section to remind you how to implement your goals, now that we have phases. If you recall, SMART stands for Specific, Measurable, Achievable, Relevant, and Timebound. Now that you have your debt in order and subgrouped, it makes setting the goals even clearer and more measurable.

Here's how we did our first goals using the SMART goals.

Today's date: February 4, 2009. By September 21, 2009, we will have paid off $1,060.

Chunk the debt, but don't just stop there. You have other tools, like your words, in your financial toolbelt to assist in your financial freedom journey!

Chapter Nineteen

(Outer Game)
THE CREATIVE POWER OF YOUR WORDS

"Death and life are in the power of the tongue,
and they who indulge in it shall eat the fruit of it."

—PROVERBS 18:21 AMPC

Words are powerful. No matter what your beliefs, you cannot deny this fact. There have been studies on the words you speak to plants and water, and how it affects them.

People have done their own experiments with plants. They speak to one set of plants with negative phrases. "You're ugly! You're worthless! You will die! You stink! I hate you!" The other set of plants get affirmations and encouragement. "You will grow. You are beautiful! You are vibrant! I love you!" Many have claimed that positive affirmations have a positive effect on their plants. They grew bigger and stronger. They were brighter. We know words have an effect on plants and people, but have you ever thought of using them on your finances?

Inspired by a story I heard from Dave Ramsey, I would walk past my debt thermometers on my fridge and say, "Debt, you're going down! This red line is going up!" Or I would say, "I am financially free!" When you talk about your debt with others, speak on positive terms. Stop saying, "Oh, I'm so broke. I'll be in debt forever!" I cringe when I hear people complain, "My student loans will be with me until I die!"

Stop it! Stop it now!

Stop professing negativity and bondage over your life! Speak the things you want to see happen. Your words are more powerful than you know! Start saying, "I'm wealthy and I live out of abundance! I am able to use my money to support my family and be a blessing to others!" What you say now and how you think about your financial situation is important for your future outcome. Being optimistic about your situation, no matter how dire, is crucial to your success.

I know managing your thoughts is a part of the inner game strategy, but I'm mentioning it here because your thoughts translate into your words. Your words morph into your actions. Actions, especially habitual actions, bring results. In addition to this, your words are a locator of where you are mentally and emotionally. I can listen to how someone is speaking and tell if they are going to be successful with achieving their goals. I can almost predict the outcome just by their word choice. As we see in the beginning of Genesis, words carry creative energy. Create with intention and speak with purpose.

Make sure your words are in alignment with your financial goals. The Bible is clear about this. "The tongue has the power of life and death" (Proverbs 18:21, NIV).

Riding the Ride: The Ups and Downs of the Journey

Slow and steady wins the race. Being able to follow your debt with either the snowball or avalanche method month by month will be the surest way to get out of debt.

But let's face it, life happens.

Life happens even though you've made plans assuming it won't. Children break bones, cars break down, the IRS comes out of nowhere with a huge bill that messes up your method. Ack! This is one of the main reasons we have our $1,000 emergency fund. So, when life does happen, we can pull from that fund to cover those unexpected expenses.

Don't get discouraged. Just cover the expense, place the money back into the emergency fund as it comes in, and get back to focusing on your method.

We've had several crazy dips during our debt journey, including blown tires, a trip to the emergency room, and vandalized cars! Though they were unfortunate, it didn't sway us or get us down. We dealt with the issue, recouped, and got back on our debt payoff schedule. You will get knocked down. That's ok.

Just don't quit.

On the flip side, just like roller coasters, there are also ups. Boy, are they fun! In the financial world, we call them windfalls. This is money, usually an amount larger than you normally deal with on a monthly basis, that comes to you unexpectedly. People think they're being tested when they go through hard times. Nope! The true test is when the windfalls come.

Money, money, money, money—*money!*

But wait. Don't get too happy yet. Windfalls of money could end up shooting you in the foot.

Many times, when people who are not disciplined with money experience windfalls, the money gets blown on crazy things. Cars. Purses. Flying scooters. Emotion takes over and logic flies right out the window. Look at the majority of lottery winners. They are usually bankrupt in three to five years, and their relationships are a mess. They're in a worse position than before they purchased the lucky ticket! There was no direction or thought about how to wisely use the windfall.

But this isn't you.

Now that you have made a decision to become financially literate and be a better steward with your finances, you've got control of these windfalls. You will know exactly how to apply them. I now see windfalls as a test of my discipline and character more than when obstacles come to challenge me. Hopefully, you will too.

The Winnings of the Wind

My husband and I were tested a few times during our debt journey. In 2010, I started submitting my creative teaching ideas to teaching contests. A few months into our debt journey, I won the Sontag Prize teaching award that came with a $3,000 teaching stipend. *What!* I was so stoked! This was not a normal part of my salary, so I could have spent it on anything. Once that check was in my hand, I could have bolted straight to the mall.

But we made a decision to be debt free.

Therefore, after we paid taxes and donated our tithes to our church, the remaining amount went to the current credit card we were targeting on our debt snowball. No questions asked. No excuses given.

Submit payment? Yes.

Then it happened again. Later that November, I was nominated for the 2010 Great American Teacher Award launched by the Ron Clark Academy (RCA) in Georgia. Out of thousands of teachers, I was selected to be in the top five. Woo-hoo! I automatically won $1,000 by being in the top five! They flew Shayne and me to Atlanta for a weekend of celebrating education and great educators. We were escorted down the red carpet lined with ecstatic RCA students cheering our names. We felt like superstars. It was amazing, and I was just joyful to be there among world-class teachers and energetic students.

Then the announcer said, "And the winner is . . ."

When I realized my name was called, I nearly fainted.

It was an honor to win that award and to share all the amazing things happening in our classrooms. As my students were celebrating with me, my debt was jumping up and down. In addition to being the Great American Teacher of the year, the sponsor of the event, Great American Insurance Group, handed me a $10,000 check—no strings attached. I have never had a check that large handed to me that wasn't already purposed for tuition or rent or some major responsibility. This was free-use money!

But we made a decision to be debt free.

So, my husband and I took that check and, after we donated tithes to our church and gave a significant amount to the charitable organizations we support, we took the remaining amount and put it against our debt. We did celebrate with a nice dinner though! Since then, I've won a few other awards that came with smaller cash prizes or some other perks. These awards are great examples of my reticular activating system opening my eyes to opportunities that I was previously not aware of. These are also great examples of God's favor and recognition of us being serious about becoming debt free.

Nevertheless, because we had a plan and were committed to following it through, that award money was applied to our debt and not spent on crazy purchases. Due to us having a plan, I believe we were favored to receive those windfall blessings.

Now you might be saying, "Well, that's awesome for you, Genein, but I'm not a teacher. I don't have access to awards and cash prizes like that!" I understand. This was just an avenue that worked for me in my field, but there are many ways to get creative to get extra funds to head your way. I'll go more in-depth about this topic in section eight. These things happen (random checks in the mail or a huge discount you weren't expecting), but, in my opinion, they happen more when you have a plan, stay positive, commit to the goal you've set for yourself *and execute.*

Chapter Twenty
(Outer Game)
THE COLLEGE YEARS: DEALING WITH DEBT WHILE IN SCHOOL

Knowing how to carry out smart financial moves earlier in life is the best position to be in. You have had less time to mess up and more time to reap the benefits of healthier choices. There are some financial strategies I wish I'd been aware of going into college. If you're past college age, feel free to skip this chapter, but if you're in college now or about to be, you certainly want to learn from my experience. Here are some areas to be aware of while you're in school.

Choose a School Based on Quality Factors—Not the Outward Brand

Schools are now branding themselves to lure students in. Like cars, schools work hard on improving their brands with amenities and components that don't really add to your overall education; the sports teams, the gym, and the high-tech dorms. Students should stay focused on the quality factors when choosing a school. Do they have your area of study? How large or small are the class sizes? Are there opportunities to explore different clubs and organizations? Is social capital (mentorship and networking) available after graduation? And the biggest question is . . .

Can You Actually Afford This School?

After you have completed the Free Application for Federal Student Aid (FAFSA) and received your acceptance letters, really analyze the amount of free money the school is offering (in grants and house scholarships) versus the amount of money you will need to borrow (in loans) or contribute from your household (expected family contribution—EFC).

Can your family afford the EFC? Calculate what those numbers will be over a four-year term. If the amount of loans you will end up graduating with is larger than your first year's expected salary, then you need to choose a less expensive school. Every dollar you take out on this side of graduation is more than a dollar you will need to pay back on the other side of turning that tassel.

Negotiate Your Financial Aid Award Letter

Negotiation isn't just for adults interviewing for a job or buying a car. Negotiation can come in handy in the financial aid office too. Some schools allow you to negotiate your award letter and possibly turn some loans into grants or merit/need-based scholarships. If your family's financial situation has suddenly changed, revisiting your financial aid package is a must. The college won't help you if you don't ask. Also, don't accept loans that you don't need. This isn't the time to buy fancy cars and go on shopping sprees with your refund check. The button to pass on accepting a loan might be tiny and wedged in the bottom corner on the Web page but find it and press it, if you don't absolutely need the loan.

Pay the Interest on Your Loans while in School

If you end up taking out loans from good ole Uncle Sam (the government), some of those loans might be subsidized or unsubsidized. Subsidized means that the government will pay the interest that is accruing to the account while you are in school. If your loan is unsubsidized, it will not. If you can afford it, ask how you can pay the interest while you are in school. It will greatly decrease the amount you owe when you graduate. Interest compounds, or grows, with time. Let it grow for you, not against you.

Don't Pass Up Free Money

Most students work hard with applying for scholarships their senior year in high school. While this is the most popular time, there are more scholarships available for students who are actually in college than in their last year in high school. Use your school breaks during winter and summer to grab this free money! Sign up for JLV College Counseling scholarship blog (jlvcollegecounseling.com) for a great list of scholarships that are sent out every Saturday! I'm on that list and you can be too!

Get a Side Hustle

I know. You're probably saying, "Genein, my whole college experience is a side hustle!" But just hear me out. Our society is going through a massive transformation. Having multiple streams of income is a necessity. While in school, see if there are any extra creative ways to bring in other forms of income. (I go deeper with this in section eight.) Can you tutor? Babysit?

Edit student essays? What are you good at? What do you enjoy doing that you could turn into income? Take a moment and reflect on your skills.

For instance, at UCLA I signed up to be a participant in various research studies. I would make money being the healthy subject in research tests and experiments. I received $60 here and $100 there. It helped. Have a plan for any extra money that comes in. Had I known what I know now, I would have invested that money or used it to pay the interest on my student loans. Instead, I just bought Skechers tennis shoes! Like cars, not a good investment at all!

Study Abroad the Right Way

College is all about new experiences and going on adventures that help you discover who you are and where your gifts are. Studying abroad is a great way to add to your experience, but if possible, avoid taking out loans to do so. While studying at UCLA, I went to Spain my junior year for the summer, and I had an amazing time. Looking back, I should have taken advantage of all the scholarships available for students to study abroad. I would not have been still paying off that six-week trip well into my thirties! So, travel! Just do it the right way, hopefully on someone else's dime!

Keep Your Transportation Budget as Low as Possible

Unless you are commuting to school, try not to have a car your first few years in college. If you're living on or near the campus, having a car might not even be necessary. You'll avoid parking and gas costs and hopefully a car payment. You might be owning a car the rest of your life, so enjoy these few years of not having car concerns and the expensive costs that come with those concerns. Most schools have carpool programs that can assist you with getting home to family. Now, with the ride-sharing economy we're in, there are several services like Zipcar, Lyft, and Uber that can supplement your transportation needs without you owning a car, and car expenses, fully outright. When I was in college, I didn't have those options, but you do!

You Can't Do It All, so Plan for What You Really Want to Do

There are so many opportunities to explore while in school and it might feel like you want to partake in *everything*. Well, because you are primarily there to study and learn your studies, you can't do every extracurricular activity, but you can and should choose the experiences that you feel you will benefit the most from. This includes experiences outside your comfort range too. Bungee jumping, anyone?

If these events come with a price tag, plan ahead and budget for them. Pay for them ahead of time if possible, rather than using a credit card. Studies show that if you plan ahead and try to prepay for the event, you will enjoy it even more.

If You Get into Financial Trouble, Get Help

College is an interesting time regardless of your financial situation, but if your finances are overwhelming you, it can feel like the end of the world. Sadly, there have been students who ended their lives due to their financial situations. Being $5,000 or $10,000 in debt can be daunting for a twenty-year-old student. Whatever your situation, if you feel overwhelmed and need assistance, please seek help.

Ask if your financial aid office hosts financial education classes for students. If you have consumer debt, like credit cards, you can also reach out to a nonprofit credit counseling service or contact the National Foundation for Credit Counseling (www.nfcc.org) for assistance. You're not alone. Get help if you need it.

Enjoy your time in school. There is no other time like your undergraduate experience. Do not let a lack of money or chaotic finances spoil your fleeting collegiate moments. If you prepare, plan, and are intentional about creating a solid financial foundation now, it will be a much easier transition when you enter your professional life and career.

Section Five Summary

1. Attack the debt with a strategy—either the snowball or the avalanche method or a mixture of both.

2. Communicate with your creditors. Most of them will work with you!

3. Chunk your debt into sections to help increase motivation tactics—go for the win!

4. Be proactive! Implement financial strategies during your college years.

LIFE AFTER DEBT: "SAVING" YOUR CREDIT

Chapter Twenty-One
(Outer Game)
YOUR SAVING GRACE

"Don't save what is left after spending; spend what is left after saving."

—WARREN BUFFETT

Debt Free—Now What?

I know you're still working on your debt journey, but let's pretend you're debt free today! Stop and imagine that feeling. You did it! Congratulations! Now it's time to continue moving your net worth number in the right direction. Calculate your net worth with no debt and admire that number. The time has come to add to your net worth by building your savings. You already have your $1,000 critical emergency fund. Now it's time to fatten that account!

Emergency Savings

A statistic that shocked America was that over 60 percent of Americans do not have $1,000 saved in the bank. Most Americans would have to put an emergency on a credit card or ask for financial help from a friend or family member. That's why, after your debt is paid, you want to start building this emergency fund to help with the blow of any "life shocks" that might come your way.

These life shocks could be as annoying as a blown tire, a job loss, a medical emergency or, they can be tragic, like a death of an income earner. Sadly, these things happen every day, so the more we can absorb the shock, the better. This is where liquid, or easily accessible, savings come in. The money that you were putting towards your debt now goes toward this savings goal. Find a money market account that has the highest interest rate possible (so you can earn as much interest as possible).

Different schools of thought have set this amount at different levels. Some say three to six months of *income* while others say three to six months of *expenses*. I have even heard up to twelve months of expenses. Another financial analyst recommends you look at the current unemployment rate and set it at that number.

For instance, if the unemployment rate is 4 percent, you should have four months of expenses in a liquid (easy to access but not too easy) account, preferably a money market account. I like this last recommendation. I also like using the "expenses" target instead of income. In the end, you really need to just cover your expenses if you are out of work.

But this total savings number should reflect your comfort level of savings. Some people feel better when they have eight months of expenses saved and others feel just fine with three months. To each his own—just have *at least* three months of expenses ready to go in case of an emergency.

Why?

Life happens!

In addition to a savings fund, another wise move is reexamining your relationship with your credit scores now that you are debt free.

Chapter Twenty-Two

(OUTER GAME) CAN YOUR CREDIT GET IT?

Credit Score Debate

As you continue to pay off our debt, you're going to reach your goal of being debt free. Yes, you will have ups and downs, but as long as you don't quit, you'll get there. All the while, as you're paying off these loans, your credit and your credit score are being affected.

Your credit score is basically your "grade" on how you handle repaying your debts. It's your trustworthiness—how trustworthy are you to pay the people you owe? There have been different schools of thought on how to handle your credit in this society.

Dave Ramsey, the creator of the Financial Peace University program, has an interesting view on credit scores. He urges people to live a debt-free life. He urges people that "cash is king." He urges people that their credit scores are no longer relevant in their financial journeys going forward. I agree with all this, except the final statement.

Yes, once you are out of debt, your goal is to live a debt-free life. While this is noble and much attainable, there are pros and cons to allowing your credit score to drop to zero. Let's face it, we live in a credit-dependent society. While I am adamant about not letting the pressures of society rule me, I am also strategic in how to "play the game" of the societal influences on my finances and on my life. Let me explain how this affects credit and the almighty credit score.

Can Your Credit Get It?

Credit is ubiquitous. It's everywhere. Not only do companies use your credit score to determine your creditworthiness, interest rates, and how much credit to offer you, but it is also used in other segments of society. When you apply for housing, on many occasions, your credit is checked. Your score might also be checked. One of my friend's grandmother couldn't get into a condo lease because she had no credit score.

In addition to housing, employers can also request to run your credit and get access to your score. Low credit scores, or nonexistent scores, can send up red flags. Some employers believe that foreclosures, multiple closed bank accounts, or liens against a candidate could be interpreted as signs of irresponsibility and negligence. If the prospective job involves handling large sums of money, employers might check your credit report or credit score to determine if you are trustworthy in that position.

Huge hits against your credit aren't the only hazards potential employers are looking for. Even minor infractions, such as constant late fees or a high utilization of credit, indicate your inability to manage your finances, and they might think these traits could also creep into your work life. Now, because you have been working your debt plan, late fees and high-debt usage should have been eliminated. Nevertheless, employers might still check.

Like employers, insurance companies can request to check your credit. Risk assessors and research studies have shown that a person's credit is a good predictor of insurance claims. This doesn't happen in every state, but the overall process of using credit and credit scores to judge character is fairly common. If you're applying for jobs, housing, or insurance, be mindful of your credit report and score. Think twice before letting your credit score drop.

Credit and Race in America

Yes, I'm going there. Whether or not it's popular opinion, race and acquisition of financial wealth have been intertwined throughout our country's history. There's no debating the negative outcomes that various policies have had on people of color's ability to achieve wealth and financial security.

For example, between the years of 1934 and 1968, the Federal Housing Administration (FHA), along with other public and private sector organizations like the Home Owner's Loan Corporation (HOLC), purposely shut out people of color from the wealth-building opportunity of purchasing a home because of the negative practice of redlining. Though FHA's purpose was to make home buying accessible to more people, this practice resulted in only 2 percent of the government-backed mortgages issued to households of color.

Most people of color could not participate in the traditional credit process, so they were forced into predatory land contracts. This led them to pay exorbitant prices, and even one missed payment would lead to eviction from the house and loss of all equity. These oppressive methods sent a destructive blow to many families of color trying to build wealth.

Credit and Gender in America

When it comes to gender, our history was not supportive. In 1974, we needed the Equal Credit Opportunity Act to make it illegal to require women to have a male cosigner when applying for credit. Just until 1981, the Supreme Court overturned state laws that gave husbands unilateral control of jointly owned property. It's only been about sixty years since women have gained ground in financial equity in the eyes of the law. So, though we have gained some ground, there is still work to be done.

Grow Your Credit

Getting out of debt is wise; ignoring your credit score is not. Use all the tools out there for financial success. You can live a debt-free life along with simultaneously growing a pristine credit score life. My husband and I have goals of becoming homebuyers or we might someday need to submit our credit reports and scores to potential employers. This score should not be zero.

Chapter Twenty-Three

(Outer Game)
LIVING STRATEGICALLY
DEBT FREE

These are my suggestions on living a debt-free and pristine credit-score life. You might or might not agree with these, but they have worked for me.

First, don't close your *oldest* credit cards. You can cut them up, put them in ice, or tape them to the top of your closet, but don't close the accounts on your oldest cards. Part of your credit score is based on the longevity of your oldest credit accounts, so if that account is still in good standing (and is paid off by now), keep it open. The cards I recommend people close are the cards that have a single use (store cards that can only be used at one store or business) and their most recently opened cards. You don't need fifteen credit cards. No one does.

Second, don't use these older cards while you are getting out of debt. Your debt snowball is sending more than enough activity to your credit report. Just keep working the program.

Third, once you are debt free, and you did your debt-free scream in your kitchen, then is the time to use one older credit card strategically. If you have iron discipline, you can use it for preplanned purchases that have already been placed on your budget beforehand. I use mine for travel purchases that we pre-budgeted. I recommend you not carry the card with you, if your discipline is not sharp. You certainly don't want to fall back into that debt trap you worked so hard to get out of. Stay focused and vigilant.

Fourth, another strategy that I have used is to place a recurring bill on the credit card. Because the credit card company threatened to close my card because there was no activity on it for a certain amount of time, I linked my Netflix account to the card. Instead of paying it directly every month from my bank, I just pay my card every month like a bill. It's a small activity, and I am paying it off before the thirty-day time limit, so there is no accrued interest. Done and done!

Now that we are climbing out of this mess, let's look to see how Americans got here and what defenses we can put up to be ahead of the game!

Section Six Summary

1. Once you're debt free, increase your emergency savings to your comfort level.

2. Just because you're debt free, doesn't mean you want a zero credit score. Live strategically debt free!

Section Seven

HOW DID WE
END UP HERE?

Chapter Twenty-Four

(Inner Game)
WE'VE BEEN TRICKED:
THE PSYCHOLOGY OF
CONSUMERISM

"Honestly, shopping beats therapy, anytime. It costs the same and you get a dress out of it."

—SOPHIE KINSELLA

Now that you have your debt snowball/avalanche method getting you to your goals, you might stop and ask, "What did I even buy?" If you have ever asked yourself this question, you are not alone.

Your numbers in your household might be disappointing, but the numbers of Americans as a whole are downright dismal. As of 2019, here are our stats as a nation.[5]

---

5   Nataly Pak. "Credit Card Debt Surpasses $1 Trillion in the US for the First Time." March 8, 2018. See https://abcnews.go.com/Business/credit-card-debt-surpasses-trillion-us-time/story?id=53608548. Janet Berry-Johnson. "What Is the Average APR on a Credit Card?" January 2, 2019. See https://www.creditkarma.com/credit-cards/i/average-apr-on-credit-card/. Lexington Law. "2019 Credit Card Debt Statistics in the US." December 19, 2018. See https://www.lexingtonlaw.com/blog/loans/credit-card-debt-statistics.html.

- Total credit card debt exceeds $1 trillion.
- The average credit card debt per person is $8,600.
- The average APR on cards is 15.96 percent.
- The average interest rate paid over twelve months is $1,183.

What are we charging on our cards?

There are three forces that are driving these numbers up. The first one, the economy, is actually an external force, so I'll mention it briefly. The other two are internal forces, which are your blueprints and consumerism. With these forces, I'll be doing a deep dive. I'll discuss various blueprints in this chapter, while consumerism is covered in the next chapter.

The Economy

Even though we're in the inner game section, I have to bring up the economy when we are discussing why people are going into debt. With the financial crash and the Great Recession of 2008, the safety nets many people had set up were suddenly wiped out from under them. Jobs were shut down, houses were lost, and any savings were wiped out. Times suddenly got really rough!

Many middle-class people, who were living comfortably with debt, suddenly found themselves without an income. Those who took the equity out of their houses for cosmetic upgrades were quickly regretting that decision. The water level of financial ruin was rising, and many houses ended up submerged, or rather, underwater. Even worse, those who had a variable mortgage saw their mortgage payment skyrocket from a reasonable amount to an unmanageable payment overnight.

With nowhere to go to pay for everyday supplies, who do you call? Who do you turn to? No, not the Ghostbusters but the credit cards. Visa and Mastercard were standing there with open arms happily saying, "Come on in!"

Along with the aftermath of the crash, people residing in certain American metro cities, such as Los Angeles, San Francisco, and New

York City, were facing substantial rising costs of living without their salaries rising at the same rate. The middle and working classes were being squeezed, and this caused their dollars not to go as far. These factors were definitely one cause of the rising credit card use among many Americans.

Though the economy might be a major player in your relationship with money, there are also some other hidden factors. Let's head back to the inner game territory—your past.

Money Blueprints

Building a house isn't a haphazard process. The builders know where each wood panel or nail goes by looking at a blueprint. Blueprints are plans that carry instructions for each action. Your actions are also directed by blueprints. These blueprints, or belief systems, were mostly drawn up during your formative years up to twelve years old. They can dictate how you respond to social situations, especially situations about money. Your beliefs shape your identity, and your identity dictates your actions. Your actions determine your results. For many of us, our results found us broke, in debt, and financially illiterate. But what were our blueprints that might have caused these results?

It's imperative that we stop and analyze our blueprints. We need to look at our past to examine what belief systems are driving our decisions and, ultimately, our actions and results. In *Abundance Now: Amplify Your Life and Achieve Prosperity Today*, authors Lisa Nichols and Janet Switzer review the different areas of blueprints that people need to be aware of.

They note, "A money blueprint is the unique combination of beliefs and actions that results from cultural, economic and other life experiences you've encountered since childhood that today influences how you make money, what you think about money, how you spend it, and how you react when money flows into your life." Getting hold of your financial health means getting hold of your blueprints about money.

Family Blueprints

The television sitcom allows you to jump into the homes of many families. Did you ever stop to think about their money belief systems? Think about the show *I Love Lucy* with Lucille Ball and Desi Arnaz. In that show, the husband, Ricky Ricardo, is the sole bread winner, and he brings home the money. He gives his wife, Lucy, an allowance with which she has to buy groceries and all the other household needs for the home. If she needs money for her hair, she has to ask him for it. If she needs money for a new dress, she needs to ask him for it. Sometimes it seems as if she was begging him. Those interactions perplexed me, but that was their family dynamic about money. Did you see this in your home? If so, this social interaction helped shaped your money blueprint.

There are families where both parents work and bring home the bacon. Both parents had access to money. Is this what you witnessed? Did your parents often argue about money? Did they ever talk about money at all? Did one parent work so much you never saw them but when you did there was always a consolation gift waiting for you? Was money used to buy love? Did your parents make sure you knew the function of work and money? Take the time to remember how the role of money played out in your childhood.

I heard a story of a woman named Teresa. She was a successful lawyer who wore expensive, red-soled shoes and carried a Louis Vuitton bag. She was a high-income earner but oddly, she always seemed to be out of money. One day, she was fed up with always being broke and sought help. Sitting down with a counselor, they backtracked to her childhood.

"So, tell me about your parents," the counselor suggested, pen in hand ready to jot down Teresa's response.

"My father passed away when I was a young teenager." She looked out the window, afraid of where the counselor was going to take this.

"Was it a sudden passing or was he sick for a while?" the counselor asked.

"It was sudden," Teresa responded. "So sudden and," she paused, "unexpected."

The counselor just looked at her, waiting for her to continue. She did.

"We were at dinner celebrating my graduation from middle school. It was a wonderful night until the bill came." She stopped to again look out the window. "I don't know what happened after that. He saw the bill and got so upset. Suddenly he started clutching his heart." Teresa brought her hand to her chest. "He kept saying he couldn't breathe."

"Was he having a heart attack?" the counselor asked softly.

"Yes. He died right there. Right next to the bill," Teresa's voice trailed off; she lowered her eyes.

"I see," replied the counselor, nodding her head, finally understanding the root of Teresa's financial problems.

Even though this story was on the extreme side, it illustrates how childhood occurrences can have a profound effect on our spending habits. Teresa unconsciously associated money with her father's death. That is why she never had any. She believed that dealing with money brought fatal outcomes, so it's best to get rid of it as fast as she could. This was her blueprint. This was driving her behavior. Once she was finally aware of this blueprint, she was able to address it and reset her belief systems about spending and saving.

In my childhood, we weren't dirt poor—but we were dusty. My single mother had to raise four children on a teacher's income. Not an easy task, but she made it work. A few times we had to "rob Peter to pay Paul," which is an expression that means you hold off paying one bill, so you had enough money to pay another bill. We would float checks and hope the utility company didn't cash them until the funds were actually available in our account. This behavior influenced my blueprint as a child. By any means necessary, get creative to keep food on the table. Make. It. Work.

Once I was a freshman at UCLA, that survivor mindset moved right along into the dorms with me. I would attend random meetings on campus, because they had decent refreshments or appetizers. Sometimes I still do that! Old habits are hard to break!

Underwater basket weaving? I'm there! Southern China chess club? Sign me up!

I even went out on a few dates just because it meant a free meal. At one time, I was working six part-time jobs (*six!*) while being a full-time student. I had to survive.

My mother taught us how to work hard, but she lacked the financial knowledge to give us solid money lessons. The money I made never stayed with me. It was all spent on random stuff—Skechers sneakers, CDs, and tapes (yes, tapes!). Investments were never taught to us, because my mother didn't know anything about them. This was a blueprint that ended up costing us the advantage of building wealth earlier in life.

Blueprints matter. Stop and reflect on how your family dealt, or didn't deal, with money in your youth. Also, be aware of the type of blueprint you are laying down in your own house. Make sure it's a blueprint that will become a great foundation for your children.

Gender Blueprints

Men and women might have various blueprints on what is expected of them when it comes to money. Just like the *I Love Lucy* example, men were expected to bring home the majority of the income, if not all of it. But today, there are more households where the woman is the higher income earner as opposed to the man. The number of households where the man is the "stay-at-home dad" has also increased since the 1950s.

Our relationship with money can be different, depending on gender. Now, this is a generalization, and everyone might not fit into this, but it bears sharing. Women tend to prefer having solid savings as a safety net. Blame it on our maternal instincts to protect our children and our households, but my female clients prefer the savings account—untouched. Some men might see money more as a marker of success or a way to help find a mate—have the high income, have the nice car, and the women will come flocking—or so it would seem.

How does your gender identity affect your money identity? If you are a woman, do you believe the man should pay for everything? Or are you singing, "Bills, Bills, Bills" by Destiny's Child, refusing to let a man pay for anything? If you are a man, how would you feel if your spouse made significantly more money than you? There is no right or wrong position to these questions. There is just the position of being aware of the effects that certain gender beliefs have on your money behavior.

These blueprints we carry also affect us in the workplace. Let's face it. Women need to deal with the gender pay gap. When many women accept positions, they are more likely to accept the first offer, without negotiating a higher salary. They are just relieved to be offered the position. Women tend to take more gender-centered jobs, like teaching and nursing, but are less seen in leadership positions and the almighty C-suite positions. Men, on the other hand, are more likely to negotiate and sometimes are initially offered higher salaries because they are men. Leadership and C-suite roles in top companies are likely to be held by men. Gender blueprints play a significant role in how we interact with the positions that pay us our livelihood.

Cultural Blueprints

The windows were open, and the warm Caribbean air was traveling through the kitchen, dancing with the sounds of laughter.

"Ya, mon, I know!" Stewart chuckled in response to the story that was just shared.

"PATA," responded Denzil, my father-in-law. Everyone laughed again. I just smiled, looking back and forth, meeting the gazes of my in-laws.

Why?

Because I had no idea what was going on.

You see, though my husband Shayne and I are both black, we are from two completely different cultures. My husband was born in Kingston, Jamaica, and I was born in Los Angeles. The first time I met his parents and visited the home Shayne grew up in, I was thrown into so many new experiences, my head was in a whirlwind. New foods, new vernacular, new games, and a beautiful new history of a people I never really encountered (except in the film *Cool Runnings*). I dived into learning more about his culture, because I want to teach our son about his history on both sides, the Jamaican and the African American sides.

Culturally, there are financial expectations that seem to permeate throughout cultural groups. Whether you label them stereotypes, generalizations, or cultural norms, they can influence the way we interact and relate to money. For instance, in the black community, it has been studied that African Americans are overactive consumers but behind the bar with investing. There is data showing our hyperactivity in the purchasing of cars with TVs in the backseat, designer clothing, and other quickly depreciating items.

In some Asians cultures, intel from some of my Asian friends, you have to be accepted into a University of California (UC) or an Ivy League school to not be considered a "failure." Being admitted into a state school (like California State University) is seen as "not making it" per some of my Asian informants. Even if you do not have the funds to attend an Ivy League school, if you get in, you go. Like Mulan, in the Disney film, you must uphold the name of the family. You must bring them honor.

An Indian comedian once noted, "If you're Indian, you're only allowed to be one of three professions: a doctor, an engineer, or a failed comedian!" Now the latter option is a joke, but you get my point. Depending on your culture, there might be certain performance expectations you might be dealing with consciously, or subconsciously, that will affect your financial behavior.

There are multiple lenses through how you see the world and how you respond to different situations. Being aware of your family, gender, and cultural blueprints will not only help you figure out why you spend, save, and invest the way you do but will also help you take initiative to create a better blueprint for future generations to come.

Let's move on to the third force to explain why Americans are charging so much on credit cards—consumerism.

Chapter Twenty-Five
(Outer Game)
THE HIJACKING OF
AMERICA'S HAPPINESS

God Bless America

This leads me to the American culture. No matter which ethnic group, which gender, or what your family dynamic was, if you live in America you are dealing with American culture. Even if you are as far away as Great Britain or Australia, our Western materialistic ways have traveled across the seas to penetrate your borders and hijack your happiness. How? Through consumerism. This is a major factor of why we are spending so much. Guess what? It didn't just happen.

It was strategically designed this way.

The Hijacking of Our Happiness

As a nation, our highest point of happiness was marked about 1950. [Now, honestly, it depends on who was polled because in 1950, black people, especially in the South, could not even drink at the same water fountain as white people. They experienced horrific, terrorizing events that would

171

greatly skew this happiness data but, for the sake of this writing, I'll use this figure.]

Americans had just ended World War II, national production was up, and people were eager to resume living in peace. Because there were new government policies being put in place to help the middle class in the areas of housing and employment, this segment of the population was booming. Most of mainstream America was happy and content.

Nevertheless, there was a problem. This problem was not with the people but with corporations.

Corporations suddenly realized Americans would stop spending once they had enough for a comfortable lifestyle. Why buy more? We're happy!

This was an issue—an issue that companies needed an expert to help fix.

Who suited up for the job? A man by the name of Edward Bernays!

The Man for the Job of Controlling the Mob

Edward Bernays, the nephew of renown psychologist Sigmund Freud, got to work right away to get people out there buying stuff. As a wartime propaganda specialist, he'd worked with presidents to move public opinion in favor of the government. Coining the term, *public relations,* Bernays had the ability to take a persuasive idea to the awareness of the public using mass media. He knew how to control people—and not just small crowds but massive groups of people. He understood that if he could get people to think a certain way during times of war, he should also be able to do it in times of peace.

Brilliant for him, costly for us.

For example, Bernays cleverly used psychology to get women to smoke, even though it was taboo to be seen smoking in public if you were a woman in those times. Likewise, he convinced Americans that bacon and eggs were the "true" American breakfast to sell more eggs. His impressive list of clients included Proctor & Gamble, The American Tobacco Company, General Electric, NBC/CBS, and even US presidents. He mastered group psychology—how people think and what causes them to act as a group—and used this understanding to persuade Americans to spend, spend, spend.

Brilliant for the companies, costly for us.

Aspirational Marketing

"How can I get people to desire something they didn't even know existed? How can I get them to long for something they are not?" These are questions Bernays pondered. He found his answers with the power of images and the power of desire.

You see, in previous advertisements, companies would just share the specifics of an item—how fast it goes, how much horsepower it has, or how durable it is. Companies would list how fast a motor was or the level of efficiency the machine offered. These advertisements appealed to logic. They merely appealed to the thinking brain. Bernays knew there was a more efficient way to get people to buy. He didn't need them to think. He needed them to feel. He needed them to desire to aspire to a higher, wealthier position.

To do this, instead of telling how the product was made, he focused on how the product made a person feel. He knew emotion was a more powerful motivator to get people to buy an item they didn't even know they needed.

+ Don't you want to be this beautiful?
+ Do you want to look this young?
+ Don't you want people to envy you?
+ Buy this!

Information was informative, but it wouldn't sway people as quickly as an emotional enticement could. Emotions move people.

Boy, was he right.

Once again, brilliant for the companies—costly for us.

True Happiness vs. Quick Pleasure

Click—snap—shhhhhhh! The refreshing sound of opening the Coca-Cola can greets you on a hot day. You take a long gulp, and suddenly you're at the beach in your perfect beach body you spent all summer sculpting. Glancing at the gorgeous people surrounding you, some on skates and others dancing, you smile. You look past them at the sunset. You feel seen. You feel loved. You feel.

Alone.

After your sugar rush leaves, you open your eyes to realize you're not on the beach. You don't have that beach body. And what about those beautiful dancers? Gone. You look down at your belly gut hanging over your belt and wonder why the joy promised in this little can didn't come through. You've been hoodwinked. So, you pick up another can and try it all over again. Maybe you said the wrong magic words . . .

Drink Happy

Coca-Cola has perfected the art of selling happiness. It has crafted the formula of giving you the perfect world you want to be in. The look, the people, the love, the experiences—everything is there. Everything except the truth.

It's actually selling you death and disability.

You know where I'm going with this. Sugared beverages alone account for 180,000 deaths per year worldwide. Sugar also ignites the aging reaction, wreaks havoc on your liver, and increases your risk for type 2 diabetes. An oversupply of sugar in our foods is one of the major reasons for increasing health costs in America. In 1980, there were fewer than ten cases of childhood type 2 diabetes; in 2019, there are thousands upon thousands of cases. The Centers for Disease Control and Prevention (CDC) made the prediction that one in three children born in the US will likely develop type 2 diabetes in their lifetimes.[6]

But Coca-Cola doesn't put this in its advertisements. There are no images of sick, obese children holding a Coke in their hand, barely able to run. There are no commercials showing you the amount of actual sugar in one bottle of Coke. It's not even on the label (as a percentage of your diet)! Nope. Just scenes of people prancing around being happy, beautiful, and free.

Emotion sells. It works. The advertisers are showing us what we want to *aspire* to, not the true effects of consuming their products. Our quest for happiness has been hijacked by companies needing to increase their profits. In return, we get a short-lived spike in pleasure, a detrimental hit to our health, suicide to our wallets, and an emotional drop in our self-esteem. It's not just with a can of soda—it's with our stuff too!

Tactics to Get You to Spend

"What's the next video on the Netflix queue?' I asked my husband, as I continued to browse the selections.

"It's the—"

Beep. Beep. I looked down at my phone. "Congratulations! You are now eligible for an upgrade! Come into your local Sprint dealer today to pick up your new phone!"

My face lit up right when I read the message. "Yea, honey! Look! I'm eligible for a new phone!" I showed him my text message alert.

"Cool!" he responded, now scrolling down the movie lists himself.

---

6   Joel Fuhrman, MD. "Sugary Drinks Linked to Hundreds of Thousands of Deaths Worldwide." May 21, 2016. See https://www.drfuhrman.com/library/ eat-to-live-blog/75/sugary-drinks-linked-to-hundreds-of-thousands-of-deaths-worldwide. Nutrition Review. "Reversing Insulin Resistance to Reduce Type 2 Diabetes." April 22, 2013. See https://nutritionreview.org/2013/04/ reversing-insulin-resistance-reduce-type-2-diabetes/.

"I wonder which phone I should get. Hmm. This one is actually—Uhhh!"

I gasped. "They're . . . controlling . . . me!" I spoke out slowly to no one in particular. I looked down at my phone. "They're controlling me," I whispered to myself.

My mind was blown. There was a disturbance in the force, in the "consumer matrix," and I felt it strongly at that moment.

Upgrade Your Life for a Price

Did your grandparents or an older relative have a cordless phone on their wall back in the day? Remember how the spiral cord was over 15 feet long and you could take the phone from the kitchen all the way into the living room? That phone lasted fifteen years! It would probably still be there if it were up to my grandmother. If that phone could stand the test of time, why do we get a new phone every year or eighteen months?

Because that is what the companies have trained us to do.

I will never forget the day I realized that phone companies have conditioned us to upgrade our perfectly good phones to purchase new ones we don't really need. Millions of perfectly good phones, along with washers, dryers, and refrigerators, are sitting in landfills all over this country wondering why they're hangin' out next to Toasty the Toaster.

Apple has perfected this process by requiring software updates that are no longer compatible with old hardware. Or the battery doesn't hold a charge after a year. When Apple came out with a recycling program to help with waste, environmentalists retorted, "Why don't you just make phones that last? How about that?" Apple doesn't want to, because it needs to increase profits year over year. So, it needs you to spend year after year. In years past, while our own net worth was going down, Apple's value was climbing.

This wasn't by accident.

"Well, Genein," you say, "I need a new phone because of the new technology." Well, that's a part of the Apple strategy. Even though it has several tech upgrades on hardware that it can launch all at once, it staggers the improvements so you will have another feature to be excited about in the near future. These are scheduled upgrades to keep you on a schedule to purchase. These are the strategic play moves, my friend. It's all a game, and we aren't the ones winning.

Once again, I'm not against cool gadgets and nice things. I just want us to be more aware of the forces behind our purchases. If your phone works just fine, and you don't need to get a new one, then don't. Be aware of the subconscious tactics getting you to buy things you weren't even planning to buy until the companies told you to buy them.

FOMO: Fear of Missing Out

It's not just with upgrade deals with phones, it's with those holiday sales too. I remember getting a Macy's coupon and seeing the commercial showcasing "July Fourth Sale—Only Two Days! Hurry in Now!" I had my coupon and was excited to see if I could find something I "needed" to buy. Unfortunately, because I went out of town, I missed the whole sale.

It didn't matter. There was another one coming around the corner.

Summer Sale. Labor Day Bonanza! Groundhog Day Sale!

There was *always* a sales event around the corner. The store just made it seem that this sale was going to be the last sale ever. It used urgency to get you into the store now. Try not to fall for that marketing trick and only go when you need an item, have a coupon, and have done your research on getting the best price.

Bought Today, Obsolete Tomorrow

Planned Obsolescence

Have you ever purchased an item and within a short time, it's not working properly? Like a cell phone that's only a year old but no longer holds a charge and needs to be plugged in constantly to use it or a high-end computer mouse that now has two buttons that don't click. You ask, "I just got this not too long ago—why is it breaking down so quickly?"

Well, this, once again, is not a coincidence. This was planned. In fact, it's called *planned obsolescence*. There's reference to this strategy in the economy journals where companies actually plan for the item to break down at a certain point of use.

Now, some companies understand that if the item breaks down too soon, you'll lose faith in not only the item but the brand—they don't want that. So, they create an item that breaks down slowly enough so you don't lose faith in the brand, but quickly enough that you will replace it with the same company when this happens. The companies have done studies to see where that exact balance point is. No matter where the points lie, they all point to separating you from your hard-earned dollars.

To combat this, you might have to do some deeper research for items that will give you your money's worth. Search for items that are well made and will stand the test of time. Look at reviews before you purchase. Don't forget. This purchase was made with dollars you traded your time and your life for, so you want them to be invested well.

Perceived Obsolescence

Companies aren't the only ones trying to get you to rotate through products quicker than need be. Your best friend is also doing it, unknowingly. If you pulled out your iPhone in front of your friends, would they gasp? Now, I don't mean the iPhone X (as of this writing, the iPhone X is the latest version) but I mean the *original iPhone*. What would their reaction be?

My friend, Tessa, had an iPhone 3 when the rest of the world was standing in line for the iPhone 6. Whenever she pulled out her phone, someone, even strangers, would comment how she was behind the times. This occurrence is called *perceived obsolescence*. Due to this social persuasion, companies intentionally change the style of their products. It's not just a design element but a perception of who is contributing to the consumer machine and who is not. Who is up to date with their consumerism? Your friends? Your parents? You?

Even though Tessa's phone worked just fine for what she needed it to do, she was "perceived" as not being cool because she wasn't up to date with her iPhone purchases.

Here's where identity comes into play. It's important to know who you are and what you believe, despite external influences. Attaching your identity to any one item or brand can be expensive, because the styles and the market are in constant motion. This constant motion urges you to keep purchasing to stay current. There are only four seasons every year on Earth but twenty-one "seasons" in the fashion industry. *Twenty-one!* The movement of the market changes so quickly, it's like being stuck on a merry-go-round. It's time to get off!

When you are secure in who you are as a person—irrespective of possessions—the movement of the market will have no internal effect on your identity. Therefore, you won't feel the need to commit to empty purchases just to stay hip in front of your peers. You'll be driven by logic rather than emotions or mind tricks. Just be you and be in control of your spending. Buy when it makes sense to replace an item and don't buy when it doesn't. Take back your control.

How to Limit Their Effects on Spending and Your Happiness

Defense! Boom! Boom! Defense! Boom! Boom!

Have you chanted that at a sporting event? Well, here is the defensive strategy to your financial game plan. True happiness takes work. It takes making a decision to be happy. You can't purchase it on a whim or put it on a credit card.

When there are forces attacking your happiness and slaughtering your finances without you even being aware, the results can be catastrophic. This is why it is important to have a strong offensive game—your debt plan, spending plan, and savings plan—and also have a strategy to defend your financial house from the psychological tricks that companies are using to deplete your funds.

Here are four strategies to place in your playbook.

1. *Metacognition—Think about Your Thinking*

I mentioned this is chapter sixteen, but I'm reviewing this tactic again because it works. Be aware of how media advertisements are making you feel. When you are aware and reflective of your mental response, you are more capable of identifying those emotions and self-correcting them. Be honest with yourself. For instance, when you see an advertisement of a slick new luxury car and you turn to look at your five-year-old Toyota and sigh, it's ok to say you wish you had a new car. It's ok to have goals. But if you are in the middle of your debt plan, you know getting a new car right now isn't wise. Remind yourself that it is just a car and does not define who you are. Remind yourself that there are billions (billions with a b) of people who have never even owned a car and would love to drive your five-year-old car. Keep it in perspective. Remind yourself that if getting a luxury car is a goal for you, it will be even sweeter and better enjoyed when your finances are stabilized, and your savings and retirement are on track.

Remind yourself of the truth and think about your thinking.

2. *Limit "You Suck" Media*

Studies show the more commercials and advertisements you're exposed to, the more your spending goes up and the lower your happiness levels are. By limiting the media you digest you are being proactive in controlling your urge to spend. You can mute the mandatory commercials that precede or interrupt YouTube videos and TV shows. Use Adblock on your other devices to block unwanted pop-up ads. Give them no more of your attention.

3. *Be Aware of Your Insecurities*

What are your coping strategies when your ego suffers a blow? You fail a test. Your significant other just wants to be friends. You didn't get the promotion.

Do you grab the credit card and head to the mall for a pick me up? Do you go shopping to dress up the outside without truly dealing with the inside? People respond differently to setbacks. But if you use money to lick your wounds, you're employing a pricey Band-Aid.

Instead of spending your woes away, practice some less expensive but healthier coping mechanisms. Connecting with someone you trust who will listen to your situation is a good route. Reflecting and expressing your feelings in a journal is also a healthy alternative. You can always give yourself a pep talk. Watch the YouTube video, "A Pep Talk from Kid President to You." It's a good one. Remind yourself that you are worthy, and you are valuable. Take your loss, learn from it, and keep moving forward.

4. *Identify Yourself as a Citizen, Not Just a Consumer*

The news even plays a part in how we flex our consumer muscle in society. We often hear newscasters mention "consumer spending," and they often refer to us as consumers instead of citizens. This is a mental tactic coaxing us to see ourselves as people who consume opposed to people who contribute, create, and are involved stakeholders of our democratic system.

Understand that our presence here on this earth and in this country is to contribute and be active in our democracy. You have a voice, rights, and an opportunity to move our nation forward. You are more than just a consumer. You are, hopefully, a productive member of our society with gifts to offer. Ignore the newscasters' attempts to solely label us as merely mindless consumers.

Using these strategies will help with advertisements from companies trying to sell you products you don't need. But it doesn't just happen at the makeup counter or the strip mall. Other organizations are trying to sell you products without you even knowing that it's a product. Where is this place? Come with me, and, like Jane and Michael from *Mary Poppins*, let's take a trip to the bank.

Chapter Twenty-Six

(Outer Game)
ANOTHER RUN ON THE BANKS

Jeff walked into the bank to make a simple deposit. He and his wife were doing ok financially—not great, but ok. Jeff headed to the teller window but Tim, from the loan department, who gave Jeff and his wife their mortgage, sees him.

"Jeff!" Tim called out. "It's so good to see you."

"Hi, Tim!" Jeff responded, heading over to shake Tim's hand.

"Have a seat for a moment." Tim walked around to the other side of his desk to take a seat. "When's the last time we spoke? A year ago, when you opened your home loan?"

"I'm not sure, but it's been a while," Jeff said, glancing at the teller window where he needed to complete his transaction.

"Well, let's see here," Tim looked down at Jeff's check. "I can take care of that for you." Taking Jeff's check and bank card, Tim started punching keys on his computer.

"Hmmm, I see you don't have a credit card with us." Tim's eyes shot up to meet Jeff's eyes. "Can I ask why not?"

"Uh, I dunno." Jeff shrugged. "I thought I wouldn't qualify for one."

"Well, I'll be the judge of that." Tim smirked playfully. "Yep! You do qualify! We can get you a platinum card with a balance of $2,500!"

Jeff's eyebrows shot up. "Really? Platinum?"

By the time Jeff left the bank, he had a credit card, a HELOC (home equity line of credit), and had opened an additional savings account.

Within a year, his family was drowning in debt and started the process of filing for bankruptcy.

Your Lucky Day

Jeff's situation isn't that unique or rare. Since the Great Recession of 2008, I started researching the truth about the *big banks* of our great US. Wells Fargo, Chase, and Bank of America are the main ones. Think about that name. Bank of America—it sounds like it is on the side of Americans. It sounds like it is required to be a part of your upward American experience. Sadly, it is not.

There have been many people who walk into banks for simple transactions and leave with more products.

Yes. You heard me right. Products.

Credit cards, loans, checking and savings accounts are actual products. When we are approved for one of these products, we act as if it is our lucky day. Don't forget that you are the client. The bank is not *giving* you a great deal but rather *selling* you a loan or a credit card. You are helping the bank reach its quota and profit goals. We often celebrate when we are approved for a loan. Banks should be celebrating that we chose them to hold our loan.

The products that banks sell are as follows.

+ Checking and savings accounts
+ Credit cards
+ Loans (mortgages, car loans, student loans, and personal loans)
+ Home equity lines of credit (HELOC)

Just like Target has laundry detergent on its shelves to sell you, banks have products on their inconspicuous shelves that they push on you. Every time I go to a Wells Fargo ATM, I am bombarded with personal student loan advertisements. When I walk up to the counter to deposit a check, the teller, without fail, asks me to open a credit card. It's constant.

No wonder most Americans are in debt. It's *in front of our eyeballs* all the time.

Customers who visit the bank to do basic transactions might be offered a financial health check. This isn't to make sure you are financially healthy. This reveals to the bank managers which products are missing from your banking portfolio so they can sell you the missing elements. Beware of these enticements. You don't want to end up like Jeff.

Your Bank Is Your Choice

You have a choice where to place your money (and under your bed should not be one of them!) but be wary of choosing *big banks*. Big banks, it seems, are now focused on profit more than people.

It was their greedy behavior that was the driving factor of the financial meltdown in 2008. While big banks got bailed out, the American people got left holding the bag. I know we need banks in order for our economy to run efficiently, but the painful recession did not have to be as catastrophic as it was. The list of scandals and fines racked up by big banks in the past decade is disheartening. They need to do better.

Banks cannot be trusted to self-regulate, as they have shown us. Policies that were in place to ensure consumer protection have slowly been reversed since the 1980s. Once again, I'm not saying all banks act in this manner, but it sure makes the entire banking industry look untrustworthy and unaccountable when some of the giant ones do. Big banks need to continue giving back to the community but also be ethically responsible to their actual customers. People before profits.

Cheers! Go Where Everybody Knows Your Name

Have you considered banking with your local credit union? Yes, one of the benefits of big banks is that they are ubiquitous—they're everywhere in every state, but now, because the presence and network of credit unions have strengthened over the years, it also makes them more accessible. The benefits and moral standards of credit unions are shining brighter than their big bank counterparts.

Here are the differences between credit unions and big banks.

+ Credit unions have members and each member is an *owner* of the credit union. Conversely, big banks depositors (you) are called customers, who have no ownership. Banks are controlled by stockholders (not you—unless you own their stock), and their primary allegiance is to their stockholders.
+ Credit unions are *nonprofit* financial cooperatives whose earnings are *paid back to the members* in the form of higher savings rates and lower loan rates. Big banks are *for-profit* corporations with declared earnings paid to stockholders only (once again—not you).
+ In the entire history of US credit unions, taxpayer funds have never been used to bailout a credit union. The 1980s savings and loan bailout and the Great Recession of 2008 used your taxpayer dollars to bail out big banks.

When you are a part of a credit union or even a small regional bank, not only do you receive better benefits, such as higher saving rates and lower interest rates, but it seems as if they go to more effort to make a personal connection.

Understand that where you bank is your choice and your choices have power. Choose wisely!

Chapter Twenty-Seven
(Outer Game)
THE CREDIT CARD: IN DEBT WE TRUST

The Tricky Psychology of the Credit Card

"What do you mean there's no money? How can you be broke? You have a Black Card!"

Athletes—our culture looks up to them. Their discipline, their skill, their commitment to the game. But they tend to have financial troubles just like the rest of us. One out of six National Football League (NFL) players end up in bankruptcy within twelve years of retiring. On the ESPN documentary called *Broke*, I heard the girlfriend of a football player be astonished that he had no more money during the off season. All she saw was his Black Card from Mastercard.

Credit card companies, which are authorized by banks, employ cognitive psychology as much as marketers and bankers. They understand the power of hitching our identities to make-believe hierarchy levels that communicate superiority and specialness. Hence, the gold, silver, platinum, and black cards. These are arbitrary labels; you could switch them out for crayon color names, and it could have the same effect.

I have the "'Pink Pugnacious Card! What's in *your* wallet?"

How do you feel when you get issued a platinum card with a high credit limit? Do you feel more important? More seen? Well, that's the point. The level of these cards is supposed to signify to others what your level of spending is, your creditworthiness, and, therefore, your perceived worth as a person.

This stratification of importance even happens at the airport. Airlines celebrate their customers who either fly frequently or hold their airline credit card. "Those of you with better cards or better flying status, you can board first!" Getting to board first is cool (gotta get that overhead bin space!), but don't forget, we're still all going to the same place. And if the plane goes down, we're all outta luck!

Now, there's nothing wrong with this from the companies' perspective—they want to celebrate their loyal customers. But, as a customer who might not have a high-status card or a billion frequent flyer miles, you need to be aware that these are tactics to get you to use their products more and/or upgrade your services. I constantly get American Airlines emails to pay money to upgrade to "Gold status" just so I can board first. Really?

Raise the Roof (or Rather Your Credit Limit)

"Congratulations! You qualify for a credit limit increase!" Oh, what joy! My credit card company sees me fit to have an even higher limit than I have now. Oh, happy day!

Not so fast.

Studies show, and the banks know, that the higher your credit limit, the more you spend. The more available credit you have on your card, the more likely you are to charge up to the top. Most people don't know that if the debt on a card is more than 30 percent of the credit limit, it negatively affects your credit score. Now, our goal is for that debt number is to be zero, but you understand.

When you have credit with banks, you have opened up communication with them. It's now a dialogue, mostly consisting of them badgering you to tack on more debt and you sending over your money to pay the bill (that you traded your life for in the form of hours worked). I would get offers like, "Spend $3,000 in the next three months to earn 3,000 miles!" and other incentives to get me to charge more on my card. Be aware of these strategic moves and act with wisdom. Just say no or, once again say, "Ain't nobody got time for that!"

Two Types of Borrowers

You would think that I would be the ideal customer for banks. I have a steady job, I pay my bills on time, and I now have a healthy net worth.

Nope.

The most profitable customer for these banks is usually the most vulnerable—those barely making it, living paycheck to paycheck. Let me show you the type of borrower banks make most of their money from.

There are two types of borrowers that banks identify.

The Deadbeat

I never thought I'd be happy to call myself a deadbeat, but, in this case, it's an honor. Deadbeat borrowers aren't favored by banks, because banks don't make money off them.

Deadbeats have these attributes.

+ They pay their balances in full every month.
+ They do not accrue interest.
+ They usually don't charge more when their credit limit is increased.
+ They still use the perks of the card (airline miles, cash back, etc.).

Like I said, I'm proud to be a deadbeat in this case. If you do use credit cards, this should be the group in which you belong. Get the perks with controlled spending, but don't pay the interest.

The Revolver

The other group is filled with borrowers living on that precarious fine line. One slip and it's downhill. Banks call them revolvers. These are the regular users who give the banks the highest profit. Banks want to retain these customers at all costs. This group usually includes low-income customers and/or customers living beyond their means.

Revolvers have these attributes.

- They pay the minimum payment every month.
- They never fully repay debt.
- They often max the credit card to the limit.
- They accrue the full interest.
- They pay extra fees—over the limit and late fees.
- They have high interest rates.
- They often use cash advances, which have the highest interest rates ever!

Just like Edward Bernays, bankers are also psychologists. They understand how to use marketing messages to get you, the customer, to open as many products as your credit will allow. Then they employ even more tactics to get you deeper in the hole.

Brilliant for them, costly for us.

This debt dialogue can start as early as when you move that high school tassel from one side to the other. Welcome to college!

A College Calamity

"Free T-shirts! Come and get a free UCLA T-shirt!" These were the announcements I heard day in and day out as I walked up the famous Bruin walk to my psychology class. Now, I'm a sucker for free items (I'm still working on that) so being able to get a free UCLA T-shirt, on my budget, was a win for me. It didn't matter if there was a tiny VISA logo at the bottom of it, I was elated! I signed up for so many credit cards to meet my Christmas list of people who I wanted to give shirts, Frisbees, and other UCLA stamped items for the holiday. I'm so serious. I really did this.

"But I don't have a job right now. Is that ok?" I asked the rep while looking over the application form.

"Sure! Just put your financial aid amount in the income section. It should be fine!" the rep said with a smile.

I remember getting my first credit card bill in the mail. I charged about $200 worth of items on the card, but when I looked at the minimum payment, it was only $15.

This is awesome! I thought. *I bought all this stuff and only have to pay $15 a month for it! Score!*

If only I had known then what I know now.

I graduated from UCLA in 2002 with over $3,000 worth of credit card debt. That freshman encounter ended up being the beginning of a long costly journey.

The New Curriculum: Credit Cards on Campus

Credit card companies specifically target college students for numerous reasons. One in four college students leaves with more than $5,000 of credit card debt. One in ten leaves with over $10,000. This is not an accident. It is an intentional move. It's moves like these that are inhibiting students' abilities to pay off student loans and build wealth for their families.

Credit card companies know that if they can foster a relationship with a young college student (who will more than likely be going into a professional career), they can gain loyalty into other products. That one credit card will lead to private student loans, which will lead to a car loan and eventually to a mortgage. The credit card companies want to grow with the student and be their sole provider of financial products. They are looking to create customers for life. Almost like a drug ring—first introduce marijuana, then add in meth, and lastly offer up cocaine.

Now they're hooked for life. They are fully dependent on drugs—I mean credit—to maintain their standard of living.

The tactics the credit card companies used when I was in school were brutal: free items, approving students who had no verifiable income or credit history, and assigning crazy interest rates. Thankfully, new laws have been passed, such as the Credit Card Accountability Responsibility and Disclosure (CARD) Act in 2009, to help assuage the effect of these banks on college campuses. These laws prohibit them from giving away tangible items, like T-shirts or Frisbees, while on campus (but they can still hand out coupons to local restaurants or credit you cash back on your credit card statement). Unlike when I was in school, they must verify income—though that is a slippery slope.

You might ask, "Why would schools allow credit card companies to target their students?" More than likely, universities receive a kickback or an administration fee, sometimes in the tune of millions of dollars, for the opportunity to market to college students. That is just how lucrative this business is. Banks and credit card companies don't invest that much money into a market that is not going to give a higher rate of return. We do that (with cars), but banks are smarter. Passing out credit cards to young gullible kids, like lollipops on a playground, is a profitable business.

Brilliant for them. Costly for us.

Let's move on to another costly move that you should be aware of.

Chapter Twenty-Eight

(Outer Game)
ID THEFT:
PROTECTING YOUR
IDENTIFICATION

You Worked Hard for It: Protect It

Another costly move is not being prudent to protect your money when you get it. When you choose a place to keep your hard-earned money, you expect it to be safe, right? Well, with the rise of identity theft, there are more cases each year of people being "taking to the bank" because of ID theft. I know what you're saying, "Genein, can you give me some good news right about now?" Yes, be alert and, hopefully, this won't happen to you, like it did me.

The whole "stick 'em up" robbery scene is so 1980s. Stealing your ID is the now preferred choice for thieves, because there is no significant jail time like there is with robbery or possession of a weapon.

Shayne and I got hit *twice* in one month from identity thieves. Someone electronically took $400 from our business account, and then someone took a check from my wallet and wrote themselves $403 for a day's work. I'm wondering what type of "work" that is, because I might be in the wrong profession!

The next week I went to represent my school at the Chamber of Commerce meeting. Guess who the guest speaker was? The Los Angeles Police Department (LAPD) ID Theft captain! Here are three tips I learned from the LAPD guru about ID theft to give you a heads-up.

1. Your mail is one of the main ways that thieves come after people. If you don't own a cross-cut shredder, get one today! Make sure anything with your name on it (even junk mail) is shredded. Thieves are even taking mail out of your trash and the mailboxes where you place outgoing mail. They use a thin stick with tape on it and "go fishing." They want your checks so they can swipe the ink and place their information on it to cash or use the routing/account numbers to electronically wipe you out.

It happens every day.

2. When you use any kind of debit or ATM card, always cover your pin with your hand when you are entering it (at the gas station, the ATM, shopping, etc). Thieves are placing little cameras nearby to record your input and, as you've heard, they can place their own swiper in the store card readers—any card readers for that matter (like gas stations, restaurants, or bars). You've seen it on police drama shows but it happens in real life too! Now the thieves have your card number *and* your pin.

Jackpot!

3. Thieves are also pretending to be company reps and calling or emailing you to "update" your account, saying they need your Social Security number and other personal info. If this happens, *don't* tell them anything (instead get their info, if you want). Hang up and then call the company's customer service number from its website or your bill to confirm the inquiry. Be wary of giving sensitive information to someone who calls *you*. Better to be safe than hoodwinked!

With all these tactics attempting to separate you from your hard-earned money, there might be instances where you become the victim of fraud, either through identity theft or bad banking practices. If you feel you have been the victim of fraud or bad business practices, please know you have rights.

Contact your state consumer protection office and file a report. You can also file a complaint with the US Federal Trade Commission Bureau of Consumer Protection.

Do your research before entering into negotiations for any financial products. Ask questions and always read the fine print on the entire document before signing it. It's best if you are allowed to take it home to review it slowly. Don't allow anyone to rush you into any contract. You always have walkaway power—use it, if need be.

You have worked hard for your money, so keeping it safe, in the best place, should be a priority.

Mental Mindset for the Win

Psychology is used constantly to separate you from your money. It's real, and it's scoring on you from all angles. Let us take the time to educate ourselves about these tactics, so we can defend ourselves in this money game. Every dollar you give to others, either legitimately or bullied from you, was a dollar you traded your time for. That dollar could have gone to help grow your net worth for your family, grown in your retirement account, been given to a cause you support, or helped your children attend college. Protect yourself, protect your assets, and protect your family for years to come. You can win!

Section Seven Summary

1. Our consumer society didn't just happen. It was planned that way.

2. Your financial behavior is rooted in your blueprints about money.

3. Be aware of the unconscious tactics used to get you to overspend.

4. Be aware of banks. Be proactive about their presence in your financial life.

5. Credit cards are slyly used to promote elitism. Don't believe the hype.

6. Protect your identity and the savings you worked hard for.

CREATIVE HEALTH FOR FINANCIAL WEALTH

Chapter Twenty-Nine
(Inner Game)
CREATE YOUR WAY
OUT OF DEBT

"Hand me that nail over there," MacGyver says calmly to the woman who is staring intently at the bomb strapped to her ankle.

Tick. Tick. Tick. Always finding himself in a tight bind, he continues to scan the area for anything he can use to diffuse the ticking explosive.

She whimpers, knowing her life is about to come to an end.

"Eureka!" he exclaims suddenly, as he stretches to grab a deflated, metallic, birthday balloon. Cutting a strip with his teeth, he wraps the metal paper around one of the wires.

"Hurry, hurry!"

Ten, nine, eight. The clock is nearing the end point.

"Just have to bring this over," he whispers to himself, as he tightens the nail under the strip. Beads of sweat fall on the ground as he pushes the final wire.

Five, four, three . . . She closes her eyes and turns her head.

Two . . .

"Here we go!" MacGyver screams, snapping the nail through the strip of metal into the bomb.

Silence.

She opens her eyes and looks wide-eyed at the frozen clock.

"It worked," she pants. "How did you know how to do that? That was really creative."

"Sometimes all you have is your creativity." He looks up at her, removing the bomb from her ankle. "Sometimes, that's all you have."

Creativity Is in All of Us

> *"Every child is an artist. The problem is how to remain an artist once he grows up."*
>
> —PABLO PICASSO

Remember those finger paintings you did in the first grade? Or you wanting to build a security contraption to protect your diary from your siblings? How about the play *Charlotte's Web*, where your sister was the main lead, but you were cast as sheep number two?

Oh, wait, those are my memories!

Nonetheless, you might have some memories where you dove into the creative arts—dancing, drawing, acting, or singing. Or times where you created an invention or innovated a new idea to solve a problem. Those adventures engulfed you in your elementary experience. You drew pictures about the tales you read. You built a catapult out of random items found under your bed. You brought funny characters to life on the stage. You sang songs that made you connect with the feelings of another. You were drenched in the creative muse of exploration. You were creative.

Then you grew up.

And it all seemed to go away.

Now we work, separate from one another in bland cubicles in boring offices. We might sing every now and then (in the shower), but we certainly don't dance. If we're giving a presentation and need to sketch a drawing, the first thing we proclaim is, "Please excuse my drawing. I can't draw." We don't attempt to solve a problem with a unique idea, due to a fear of what others might think.

Gone is the gleeful abandon of creating. Gone is the beauty of developing something to share with the world. Gone is our imagination.

The Cost of Creativity

> *"In order to create, in economic terms, you absolutely need a vibrant living effective imagination."*
>
> —Rabbi Daniel Lapin

"Well, Genein," you ask, "why are you talking about this now? How does creativity connect to my finances?"

I'm glad you asked!

Look around you. Seriously. Put down the book or your device and look up, to the left and to the right. I'll wait here until you're done.

(Cue background elevator music.)

So, what did you see? Colorful light fixtures? A projector? A neon sign? A flat-screen TV? Whatever you saw, guess what? Someone created it. There was no puff of smoke and suddenly it appeared. It didn't just manifest itself into physical form. It started as an image in someone's mind. Someone saw it in their imagination and then through a series of steps—through a creative process—they put it together.

They created it.

Our imagination is an integral part of our financial health because from our imaginations is the birthing of our ideas, our inventions, and our ability to recognize opportunity—and, therefore, our ability to make money. Utilizing our creativity isn't just for five-year-olds playing with blocks in the kindergarten classroom. It isn't just for those group of kids dancing on the stage singing Disney Broadway songs.

It's for you.

Creative thinking is the key that opens doors to a whole new realm of possibilities. Take the internet, airplanes, and automobiles, for example. The opportunities that resulted from these single creations were massive. These separate inventions sparked the birth of entire industries.

Your creative idea could be next!

What Is Creativity?

I have come to the realization that the term creativity has been intermingled with the concept of artistry. Now while I believe having a strong foundation in artistry is important, it is not to be equated solely with creativity.

Creativity has three components—value, relevance and novelty.

Value refers to the importance it carries for the creator and the audience. This is a subjective measurement, but if you are creating something for an intended market or buyer, you must be able to demonstrate its value.

Relevance refers to the degree by which the solution actually solves the problem at hand. If you are creating an answer to a problem, and that answer is not relevant to the actual problem, then the answer is useless.

Novelty refers to the originality of the solution. MacGyver was skilled in having novelty in his solutions. His idea was unique yet relevant and therefore creative. Creativity is more than artistic creativity but, as an artist, I believe education in the arts background can enhance your creative thinking in non-art areas, including your financial journey.

Everywhere you look is the result of creative thinking. Now it's time to reconnect with your own source creativity.

Chapter Thirty

(Inner Game) CREATIVITY: YOUR MOST IMPORTANT SKILL

"Creativity will become the third most important skill in the workforce by 2020."

—WORLD ECONOMIC FORUM

Developing Creativity Is a Must

As our society continues to evolve and new technologies are quickly taking the place of human workers, more and more discussions are arising on raising "robot-proof" children. Basically, how do we keep robots from taking the jobs our children were supposed to be doing? Well, that might not happen but, with artificial intelligence, robotics, and other technology advancements, we still need to be cognizant of the "future of work" shift that is happening all around us.

No longer are we in the industrial or manufacturing economy. Gone are the days of large US factories and the assembly line most of America's middle class mindlessly interacted with like cogs in a machine. We are now in the information and imagination economy. Basic knowledge is no longer enough. I have always advocated that creativity training and the creative arts are an essential part of the human experience and especially a part of a child's education. Now, it's not just essential, it's mandatory.

With the advent of artificial intelligence and automation, it's imperative to foster creativity as a competitive advantage. Jobs that involve creative thinking are less likely to be automated. The future belongs to those who celebrate and develop a different kind of mind—a mind that is grounded in creativity, emotional awareness, and intuition.

With these creative opportunities, we'll need people who are able to adapt and modify their methods in new situations. People who can generate ideas and execute them to develop something new and valuable will be the driving force of society. Could you be that person?

Benefits of Thinking Creatively

Even though everyone is born creative (yes, this includes you!), we still need to intentionally exercise our creative muscles through every phase of our lives. Just like learning a language—either use it or lose it! If we are intentional about growing our creativity, the benefits are endless. In his book, *Originals: How Non-Conformists Move the World*, Adam Grant talks about the advantages of having exposure in the arts and how it enhances our abilities in other areas, such as business and making money.

He states, "Interest in the arts among entrepreneurs, inventors, and eminent scientists [. . .] People who are open to new ways of looking at science and business also tend to be fascinated by the expression of ideas and emotions through images, sounds and words [. . .] The arts also serve in turn as a powerful source of creative insight."

Highly creative adults use their artistic experiences within the arts to enhance or support their entrepreneurial money-making skills. When we think and examine the world with a creative eye, we are able to (1) engage different perspectives of the familiar, (2) connect the unconnected, and (3) gain introspection on our own skills and contributions.

Creative Perspectives

I have spent over ten years teaching creative arts integration. Watching students combine the arts into other subjects to communicate their knowledge is exciting, because I see them interact with the material in a whole new way. For instance, my students created a music piece to show their understanding of the relationship between two main characters in a story they were reading.

Music served as an entry point into the literature. Analyzing the story with a newfound depth and perspective helped them pull out new information that was always there but hidden. The revelations pulled out of the literature through questioning, analysis, and interpretation are usually much more profound than if they had just read the text and responded to the questions on a worksheet.

This didn't just happen with my students; I also experienced it. In addition to teaching elementary music, I also taught an arts integration course for teachers who were getting their master's degrees at California State University, Northridge. They had to do a final creative piece presentation, so I decided to do one too. I choreographed a dance showing the relationship between the spider, Charlotte, and the pig, Wilber, in the story *Charlotte's Web*.

Now, I have interacted with that story many times throughout the years. I've read it twice and seen multiple movie versions. Nevertheless, it wasn't until I had to create a dance piece and deeply investigate their development as individuals and as friends, that I realized the significance and power of Charlotte's words she used to describe Wilber.

In the story, Wilber is a pig who is in danger of being slaughtered. Charlotte, a barn spider, devises a plan to save Wilber and weaves words into her web so the farmers will see these words and spare Wilber's life. She had to strategically choose the right words and place them in the right place.

Charlotte didn't just choose any words to place over Wilber. She chose words that spoke to who his character was becoming. At the beginning of the story, he was timid, unsure, and fragile but as Charlotte began weaving these powerful words over him—Some Pig, Terrific, Radiant, Humble—he slowly transformed into what she declared. He took on that new identity—his true identity. Wilber grew into the vision that Charlotte had for him.

This revelation would not have presented itself so clearly to me had I not expressed my understanding through dance. It made the story even more poignant for my audience of students and for me.

> *"The only limit to your impact is your imagination*
> *and commitment."*
>
> —TONY ROBBINS

Perspective: A Financial Revelation

Believe it or not, our finances are the same way. First, after we make our decision to become financially free from debt and financial stress, we need to see our situation with new eyes. We need to get creative with it (instead of just gettin' jiggy wit' it). I'm not saying you have to dance around with your debt number or write a song about your financial freedom, I'm just advising you to see things in a new, creative way.

No amount you're dealing with is impossible to overcome. It all depends on how you see it. We call this framing the problem. Shayne and I had almost $100,000 worth of debt, and though that number was scary to us at first, when we changed our perspective and got creative with how to handle it, our finances became a game that we were determined to win.

But like my revelation with Wilber and Charlotte, I realized this was deeper than just Shayne and myself. This was worse than just credit card interest. This was more than just our $100,000 worth of debt and bad financial decisions.

This was an epidemic.

This was a national tragedy.

Debilitating student loans, lack of financial literacy, and nonexistent investing didn't just affect the Letford household. It was also sabotaging millions of Americans' future hopes and dreams. My eyes were opened to the inconvenient truth that my generation, and those following closely behind us, were up against.

So, with this new perspective, this new frame, I attacked our financial situation with a vengeance, and then I went out to help others tackle their financial messes. Public speaking, workshops, coaching, online courses, and books were the result of me looking at my own financial situation with a new creative perspective. I had no idea all these skills were latent inside me, waiting for a chance to fully blossom in the service of financial and creative education.

Now, I ask you, what is latent inside you? What skill, talent, or passion is waiting patiently to blossom into a solution or possible revenue source? Are you ready to do the work, the creative work, to find those opportunities?

Chapter Thirty-One
(Inner Game)
THE CREATIVE WORKOUT: GETTING BACK TO YOUR CREATIVE SOURCE

Connecting the Unconnected

Training in the arts, and especially arts integration, allows us to see connections between fields that are not normally connected. Another reminder: even though creativity isn't solely artistry, creativity can be greatly enhanced through artistic training. Do you love the fonts on your computer? Those came to be because Steve Jobs, the founder of Apple, popped into a calligraphy class during his short time in college. Combining computers with artistic writing was the perfect example of crossing separate concepts from two different disciplines to form a much-needed typeface for word processing that is common to us today. This is a perfect example how artistic training can increase our creativity in non-artistic fields.

When it comes to our finances, being able to connect the unconnected can result in additional income or opportunity. We first have to be open to opening our eyes and be sensitive to our surroundings.

"If you love sleep, you will end in poverty.
Keep your eyes open, and there will be plenty to eat!"

—Proverbs 20:13 KJV

Through the Mirror of My Mind: Introspection

Discovering new perspectives and connecting the unconnected both complement the gift of introspection.

Ask yourself these questions.

+ What do I enjoy?
+ What was I good at as a child?
+ What do I excel at as an adult?
+ What are my areas of expertise?
+ What problems can my gifts and abilities solve?

In addition to asking yourself these questions, have close family members or friends answer those questions about you. What qualities do they see in you that could be parlayed into a service?

After my husband and I made our decision to become debt free, we had to think about additional ways we could increase our income to increase our cash flow and knock out our debt faster. I made a list of all the things I enjoy, the things I do for income, and the things I do for fun. My list included the following items.

+ Creating engaging lessons for arts integration
+ Teaching/Tutoring
+ Photography

- Videography
- Speaking
- Writing blogs
- Odd jobs to help assist productions
- Karaoke

This was my list. And lo and behold, I realized I could transfer some of these activities into income streams. I tutored on the side. A colleague loved my school photography, so she asked me to photograph her son's baptism. A church friend loved the mini highlight wedding video I made for them, so she asked me to film her student dance productions. I got my first paid speaking gig and received my first book contract. I shared my creative teaching methods and won a few monetary awards. Had I not stopped and made time for deep introspection, I don't know if I would have been as focused to utilize my skills to bring in extra income.

Don't forget to interview your family. When I went to my family members to get their insights about my skills, my sister, Genae, said, "Genein, we know you're a teacher. But what you really do well is break down complicated concepts so anybody can understand them. That's a gift. And with finances, you make it seem likes it's not so bad. People need to feel that. They need hope about their situation. You give them that hope."

That was a wonderful thing for her to say, and it made me more confident that I could teach financial literacy along with creative literacy. My professor mentor also offered me a position to teach an art integration college course for teachers obtaining their master's degrees. Teaching at the collegiate level was *never* on my goal list. But, once again, when you get focused on a goal and do your part, opportunities come and find you. They chase you down! God blessed me with that collegiate position, and it really helped eradicate that last part of my student loans while giving me the credibility and experience I needed to become a creative expert.

Other examples of combining passions with entrepreneurial pursuits started popping up everywhere I looked. I heard of a man who fused his love of museums with theater to start a side business that brought artifacts to life for museum visitors. Museums can be construed as boring to some people, so he came up with a creative idea to that problem. He would be a personal tour guide and animate the various exhibits with his gift of storytelling and acting. This is a perfect example of combining creative skills with financial abundance.

In my situation, all of these income sources were not previous income sources until I thought differently about them. Using multiple perspectives, being introspective, and connecting the unconnected helped Shayne and I move the needle faster. This is a time for you to analyze your skills, hobbies, and talents to determine if they could possibly become income streams to assist your debt payoff journey.

So now that you know my experience, what are some skills, talents, or jobs you can brainstorm that might bring in extra income? Write your list here.

Creative Talent/Skill	Possible Ways It Can Bring in Income

"Each problem holds for you a gift in its hands.
You seek problems because you need their gifts."
—RICHARD BACH

Exercise Your Creative Muscles

Creativity is a muscle. Just like our physical muscles, if you don't use them, you lose them (well, maybe not fully lose it, but it can become weak). While our consumer muscle is overdeveloped, as adults our creativity muscle could use some tender loving care (TLC). To see things differently, we need to get in our creative gym and exercise our creativity!

I teach entrepreneurs and other professionals how to expand their creative thinking in my Creative Wealth Academy program. Here are a few of my favorite activities.

How Many Uses?

In Malcolm Gladwell's book, *Outliers: The Story of Success,* he suggests that intelligence, though important, only matters up to a certain point. He claims there are other factors that start to matter more, once a certain level of intelligence is met.

To exercise this point, take the following challenge called the 'Guilford's Alternative Uses Task'.

Grab a blank piece of paper and write down as many different uses you can think of for the following object in three minutes.:

1. A brick
2. A blanket

How did you do? How many did you write down? Were your ideas similar, or did you have ideas that were distinct from one another.

In Gladwell's example, he examined two students participating in this challenge. One student had a variety of sixteen answers that ranged from practical uses to illegal uses to violent uses, such as breaking a window to escape. The other student (who had a higher IQ) only listed a few uses for the brick, such as building things and throwing it. For the blanket, he listed keeping warm, smothering a fire, and use it as a hammock and a stretcher.

Now, when you are looking for imaginative ideas, which student would you want to work with?

People who practice and develop their creativity have a fertile mind that will spur more ideas and connections that could bring in addition income. Be aware that creative thinking has less do with academic intellect and more to do with experiential learning. This means the more experiences you have to draw on, the more resources you can pull from for creative thinking. Your creations are shaped by experiences and how you perceive the world. Experiences matter. Exposure matters.

What Do You See? Creativity Drawing

I enjoy doing this activity with students at the beginning of the semester. Using these three lines, draw a picture incorporating all the lines, however you see fit.

What do you see?

After all my students have completed their drawings, we turn our classroom into a walking creative museum and view other drawings.

The students were amazed that everyone started out with the same starting point—three lines—but ended up with different outcomes. Each person had his or her interpretation and perspective to what it could be, to the possibilities of those three simple lines.

I also do this exercise with my students with items around the classroom or the house. Pick up a pencil and say, "This isn't a pencil. This is a _____." Fill in the blank with another object from your imagination. Explain its usage. Acting it out is even better. This gets my students to abandon the original use of the item and extend its features for a completely different use. The more creative the imagined item, the more unique the function.

The Vulnerability of Creativity

Now, when you start to strengthen your creative muscle by doing these exercises and developing loopy answers to the game questions, it might seem odd and you might feel silly. You might have not done exploration activities like this since elementary school. If you're in a group, you might feel embarrassed or shy to offer some off-the-wall answers because of the fear of being laughed at. Well, let me tell you this.

Let them laugh.

Some of the best ideas came from initially crazy ones. Great ideas don't just fall in your lap. They don't just show up. They are uncovered. They are developed. They build on previous ideas. Bit by bit and piece by piece.

For that to happen, some crazy ones have to come out. You have to be vulnerable enough to dig deep to see what's really there. In the words of the musician Seal, "We're never gonna survive unless, we get a little crazy!"

> *"If you want to improve, be content to be thought foolish and stupid."*
>
> —Epictetus

There are so many creative activities you can do with yourself, your peers, and/or your children. We do a deep dive through these ideas in the Creative Wealth Academy. We help you expand your mind's capacity to think beyond what you see, beyond the norm, and into the imaginative realm of possibilities. Work out that muscle in this "creative gym," so it will be strong in the actual environments where opportunities and financial abundance can be uncovered.

The Creativity Ball Is in Your Court

Creative thinking allows you to take control of your financial journey. It's time to be a proactive participant in your financial freedom. I personally believe God uses our creativity and imagination as an entry point to spur ideas that can bring financial resources for our purposes in life.

But there's a catch.

We have to do the work. Many of us have creative ideas, but few actually take the initiative to do anything about them. People want to be financially free but don't want to do any work. They forget that their innate gifts, combined with learned skills, need to be hitched to the wagon of committed action. Take initiative. Be proactive.

Brainstorm ideas—a bunch of ideas! Out of the many crazy ideas, there will be some good ones that pop through. From those good ideas might be some great ideas. Who knows? From those great ideas just might be your million-dollar idea worth investing in.

Section Eight Summary

1. Your financial wealth is affected by your creative health. Having a robust imagination is key.

2. Practice connecting the unconnected and looking at situations through various perspectives.

3. Creativity is like your biceps. You have to work them to get stronger.

BUILDING WEALTH
WITH INVESTMENTS

Chapter Thirty-Two

(Outer Game)
INVESTING TO
BUILD WEALTH

"Do the difficult things while they are easy and do the great things while they are small. A journey of a thousand miles must begin with a single step."

—LAO TZU

Investing for the Future

While using your creativity to deal with the debt and save for your emergency fund, investing can be the next area of focus. Remember, the goal is to build wealth for ourselves, our families, and eventually our communities. One of the first places we are going to start to invest in is us.

Remember the "old" Genein we met in chapter one? Well, she would love to be able to be above a basic need threshold in her old age. She would love to have decent food, housing, healthcare, and enjoy some light travel. But if old Genein is not able to work anymore, she needs another source of income. This income, ladies and gentlemen, is called retirement or *investment income*.

Now, some people continue to work during retirement, some don't. Some must and some just won't. Whatever your situation will be, please begin to think about the "winter season" of your life. This is when springtime has passed. The strength and innocence of your youth has faded. Dark spots now adorn your limbs, and you have no idea how they got there. (Yep, there's another one!)

Yes, the winter of your life is coming. This is the time when you are unable to bring in an active income (trading time for money). This is the time when you should be financially independent, which means living off the interest of your *personally invested* resources. It's like the Energizer Bunny magically puts a monthly salary in your bank account every month to live off without you working for it. Wouldn't that be wonderful?

If you get your finances in order now, you'll be ready. Believe me, this time is coming.

Hole in the Bucket: Social Security

Some young people I've met aren't that concerned about getting ready for retirement in their younger years.

"Well, Genein," they say, "I'm paying into Social Security and that should be enough, right?"

Wrong.

I'll spare you the full historical background of Social Security, but basically it was started as a part of the New Deal policy when most Americans had a life expectancy of sixty-five years. People were expected to be dead by the time Social Security kicked in. Genius!

But wait. We have a problem now.

People are living well into their eighties and nineties. Along with a longer life expectancy, medical costs are rising, so expenses for a retired person are rising also. Retirees need to have enough money for healthcare costs *and* enough money to last the duration of their lives. If you retire at sixty-five but live to the ripe old age of ninety, that's *twenty-five years* of money you will need to have saved up. Many elderly people are concerned about outliving their money. If they have anything saved at all.

My fellow teachers' life spans are even more impressive. Teachers, compared to other professions, live the longest, and female teachers outlive them all. As of now, in 2019, many teachers have a pension (guaranteed income for life) but many other professions do not. Saving for your retirement is fully dependent on your tenacity to be disciplined with your money. This segment of your financial journey needs to be dealt with, with intention, and the sooner the better.

If investing for retirement is not intentional, you are, by default, expecting Uncle Sam to take care of you. Let's see how our government is doing as of 2019.

The American government has over nineteen trillion dollars of debt. Nineteen trillion dollars in debt! Our Social Security, which once had more workers supporting a smaller number of retirees is lopsided now. We're upside down actually. Due to the Baby Boomer generation, which is living longer, we now have *fewer* workers supporting *more* retirees. This system cannot be sustained.

Is this the system you're putting your faith into?

Even if you are confident in the Social Security system, if you are forty or younger as of 2019, it might not even be useable by the time you're ready to retire. But let's say it is. The average Social Security check is $1,200 a month. Can you currently live off $1,200 a month? Then add in additional healthcare costs and—well, you're starting to see my point.

But there's a light at the end of this tunnel, because you are being intentional about improving your finances today. You're being intentional about making better choices. The "old you" is depending on today's you to act!

Chapter Thirty-Three

(Outer Game)
THE CHICKEN OR THE EGG DILEMMA: DEBT VS. INVESTING

"Those who understand interest earn it, and those who don't, pay it."

—ALBERT EINSTEIN

In many of my workshops and seminars, I always get this question, "Genein, I know investing is important, but should I be investing for retirement even if I have debt?" There are many opinions about this question. Dave Ramsey says no. Other financial gurus say yes. In the end, you need to do what you feel is right for your situation, but here is my position on the matter.

What is the most powerful factor with investing?

Rate of return? The dollar amount invested? Time?

With all my studies on this, I personally believe it is time.

Yes. *Time!*

We spoke about that word when we discussed how, when earning active income, every dollar that leaves your pocket was a trade for your time. Now, with investing, every dollar that leaves your pocket has time to supersize because of the magic of compounding interest.

Yes, my friends! Compounding interest is a beautiful thing.

It's better than froyo, candy corn, or even sliced bread. Albert Einstein has even been credited with saying it is the eighth wonder of the world. It's just as beautiful as the Grand Canyon or Niagara Falls. Not really, but you get my point.

Though I'm not going to go into the deep math, I will give a few examples of how compounding interest can work with your money. Here's one example.

Would you rather have . . .

1. A check for $100,000 right now?
2. A penny that doubles every day for the month of May?

Think about it.

Our first response is to take the check, because it is a large sum of money! It's immediate. It's free money, right now! It's more than we've ever had at one time! Yet, if you truly understood the power of compounding and the power of time, you would reconsider your answer. Check out the graph below.

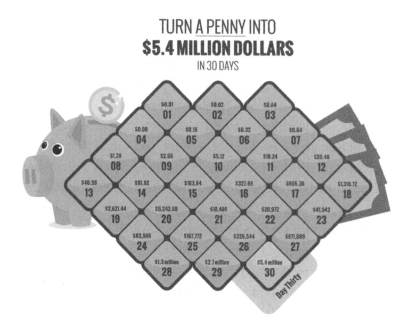

Look at the first half of the month. Not too impressive. Yet, if you have the fortitude and patience to wait, the payout of a doubling penny is amazing! However, you have to invest the time for the doubling to take effect. You have to employ delayed gratification and let the penny do its magic. The best magic happens later in the month, about day eighteen. Look out! The compounding effect really starts popping about day twenty-seven. Pop, Pop, *Pop*!

Your investments follow the same concept, more or less. They have the opportunity to double if given the right conditions, the right return, and a good amount of time. Once again, I'm not going into the deep math but watch "The Rule of 72" video on YouTube to get a better understanding of this concept.

Because no one is actually walking around trying to double your pennies, here's a real-world example to further cement why you want to invest *earlier in life*.

Let's say you started investing at twenty-five years old. You only put in $83 a month for a total of $1,000 a year and stopped at thirty-four years old. The grand total invested was $10,000 over that ten-year period. You just left it there. Not too crazy, right? There's plenty of young adults who could put $83 into an investment account for ten years.

By the time you were ready to retire at sixty-five, considering your account had an 8 percent return on the account, you would have $157,435 in your account! This is due to compounding interest and the amount of time that interest had to compound. You only put $10,000 in the account and ended up with over $150,000! Once again, *this* return on investment is much better than a car's return on investment. Much better.

Yet, what would happen if you waited ten more years to start investing and you were thirty-five? At thirty-five, you put in $83 a month for, not ten years, thirty years. You started at thirty-five years old and stopped at sixty-five. You put in a total of $30,000 over the thirty years you were investing. With this larger amount, you should have more money, right?

Wrong.

You would only have $122,346 in your account by the age of sixty-five!

This is the ultimate effect of how time is a critical factor of investing. The stock market will go up and down. That's what it's supposed to do. Bears will sleep, and bulls will charge (stock market humor). Yet, if you have time on your side, you can endure the roller coaster ride of the stock market and the "old you" will be mighty grateful you started early. No worries if you are getting this information a bit late. My favorite quote is this proverb.

> *"The best time to plant a tree was twenty years ago.*
> *The next best time is now."*
>
> —CHINESE PROVERB

So, if you are still working on your debt plan, let's see when the best time is to start investing.

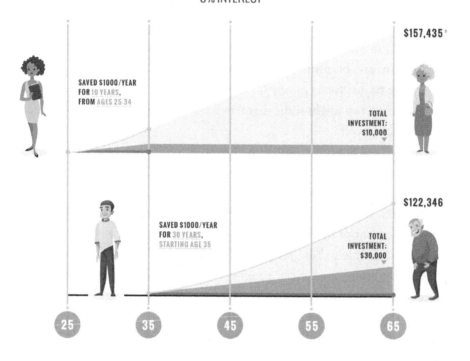

THE POWER OF COMPOUNDING INTEREST
8% INTEREST

$157,435

SAVED $1000/YEAR
FOR 10 YEARS,
FROM AGES 25-34

TOTAL
INVESTMENT:
$10,000

$122,346

SAVED $1000/YEAR
FOR 30 YEARS,
STARTING AGE 35

TOTAL
INVESTMENT:
$30,000

25 35 45 55 65

Dump Debilitating Debt

Now that we understand that time is of the essence, how does this play into your financial freedom journey? By now, you have saved $1,000 for an initial emergency fund and started working on your debt snowball/avalanche method. Once you ordered your debt by either balance and/or interest rate, you directed all your extra income toward that debt, including the previous payments of paid accounts.

Now, look at your debt. How many accounts do you have that can be classified as debilitating debts? That's my term for debt that carries a high interest rate. There's no sense in investing in a retirement account that is earning 6 percent or 8 percent, if you are paying the minimum payments on credit cards that are charging you 18–24 percent. You're running backward! And as a UCLA former track and field athlete, let me tell you that it is impossible to win any race running in the *opposite direction!*

If you can get rid of all your debt within a relatively short amount of time, go all in and just focus on becoming fully debt free. Depending on how old you are, becoming debt free within three to five years is a doable time frame to just focus purely on the debt. But if your debt will take you over five years, you might want to start investing before you have completed the full debt payoff.

In our case, we did resume our investing *before* our final debt payoff. Here's how our numbers looked and why we chose to invest *before* doing our debt-free scream.

In 2009, we stopped *all* investments. That was the time I hit my rock bottom moment of holding my Bank of America bill in one hand and the $60,000 student loan bill in the other hand. We both were thirty years old. We quickly found a financial program called Financial Peace University and got to work shoving all our extra money directly to our debt. The money in our retirement accounts was left alone to continue growing. We did not withdraw any of our retirement funds to pay off debt. I suggest you don't either.

Once we got rid of all our debilitating debt in 2012, which included our credit cards (15–27 percent APR), and Shayne's car (7 percent APR), we just had my student loans left. The APR on my student loans were, thankfully, only 3.3 percent but I still had $40,000 left to pay off. Nevertheless, we had to make a tough decision. Do we still focus 100 percent of our extra money to this debt or do we move a small amount of money a month toward our investments?

Knowing how valuable time is with compounding interest, I didn't want to let more time pass us by. We were both thirty-three years old by then. So, we went back to investing a minimal amount into our investment accounts and directed all our other funds to my student loans. Once we were debt free, we kept investing that minimal amount while we built our full emergency fund. Once that fund was built up, we increased our investments to 15 percent of our gross income.

Of course, there are pros, cons, and opportunity cost factors to consider, but I'm glad we got back into the stock market when we did. Stocks were still coming back from the Great Recession of 2008. Had we waited until we were fully debt free at the end of 2015, we would have missed out on three years of growth from 2013–2015. The student loan APR of 3.3 percent ended up being smaller than the return on our investments, which was hovering about 8–9 percent. So, it was worth it, and we still got to our end goal of being debt free.

Chapter Thirty-Four

(Outer Game)
INVESTMENT HACKS

Taking That First Investment Step

Most people don't invest, because they have no idea how to get started. They don't know what to look for or which questions to ask. So, they avoid it all together. Don't let this be you. Get informed, and once your financial journey says it's time to invest, start. You can begin after you are fully debt free and your emergency fund is set, or maybe a little earlier, depending on your situation. Just make sure there is a start date.

This isn't a comprehensive investment book, but I will offer you a few tidbits to get you thinking about your investment strategies while you are getting a handle on your debt. At the end of this book, there is a reference list of investment books to help you further your self-education with investing. Let's start with the individual retirement account (IRA).

1. Ask your employer if the company has a 401(k) match program. This means it will match your investment contribution up to a certain percentage. If the company does, you want to get the match as soon as possible. For example, if you make $3,000 a month and the company matches up to 5 percent, if you contribute $150 of

pretax money (Uncle Sam hasn't taken his share just yet), the company will put in another $150 on your behalf. That's 100 percent return on your money! Free money! So, get through your debilitating debt and then contribute to your 401(k) investment up to the match. Use the rest of your money to finish paying off your lower-interest debt.

2. If your employer does not have a match program, go to an investment firm and open a Roth IRA when your debilitating debt is paid off. This type of IRA investment account takes after-tax money. This means the money you put into a Roth IRA has already been taxed from your paycheck. It should be in your personal bank account before it moves into the Roth investment. As of 2019, to add to a Roth IRA, your income has to be lower than $135,000 for single filers and $199,000 for married couples. Choose a simple target date for the fund, based on when you would like to retire, and contribute a modest amount every month.

3. When choosing an investment firm, please check the fees! In my opinion, fees should not be more than 0.5 percent for a digital investment and no more than 1 percent for human managed investments. Here's a graph to show you how fees can eat up your returns—which is your money, which is your time, which is your life!

ASSUMPTIONS:

Starting salary:	$40,000
Annual raises:	1 percent
Annual return:	4 percent
Annual savings:	**6 percent of salary**

ESTIMATED BALANCE SAVED AFTER 30 YEARS

2019 dollars, in thousands

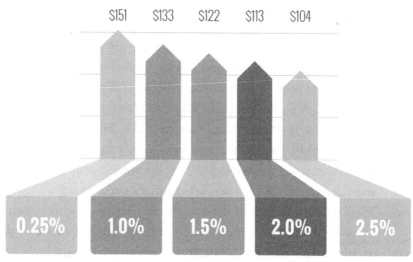

$151 $133 $122 $113 $104

0.25%   1.0%   1.5%   2.0%   2.5%

TOTAL FEES

Returns and salary growth rates are both adjusted for inflation, making the balances in 2019

Source: Vanguard

4. Check your accounts regularly. A good time is at the end of each quarter when you track your net worth. The amount might go down once in a while. Don't freak out! This is the stock market. Nothing is guaranteed, and there is risk. But unless you're retiring within the next year or two, you don't have to worry about the ups and downs of the stock market too much. Just contribute consistently and leave your money in place so it can grow. We want it to double, but remember, that takes time. Once you are debt free, finish building your emergency fund. Then return to your investments and increase your contributions to 15 percent of your gross income, if you are able. That would be $450 a month of a $3,000 gross monthly income. When you get a raise, give your investment contribution a raise too!

5. Do further research if you would like to put your money into a tax advantage account—like a 401(k) or 403(b)—or stick with an after-tax account (like a Roth IRA). There are pros and cons with each. One retirement method I agree with is to contribute up to the match at your company (like a 401(k) or 403(b) account), then max out your Roth IRA (as of 2019 you can only contribute up to $5,500 a year if you're under fifty years old—$6,500 if you are over fifty years old). Then if you have more money to contribute to your retirement, go back to your pretax account with your organization and put as much as you can there until it's maxed out.

6. "Genein, how do I know if I'm on track?" This is another question I hear often. For most of us who started behind the ball, either due to debt or lack of information at an earlier age, it might seem as if we will be playing catch up. That's ok, just start as soon as it fits in your financial journey. For those who are younger and getting this information sooner, these targets might be more realistic to shoot for. Here's a quick retirement target for you.
    By the time you are thirty years old, a savings target is one times your starting salary.

By the time you are thirty-five, it should be two times your starting salary.

So, if you started at $50,000 a year, by the time you were thirty-five years old, your target is about $100,000 saved in a retirement account.

By the time you are fifty years old, your target amount is six times your starting salary.

When you are ready to retire, your target is ten times your starting salary.

SAVE "X" YOUR STARTING SALARY

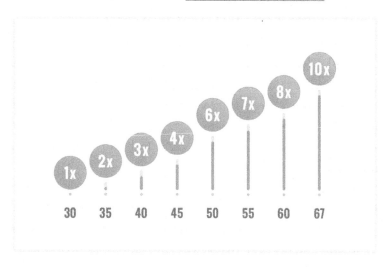

Now, there a lot of people who are nowhere near these targets, but it helps to see, in a perfect, debt-free, financially healthy, and equal justice world, what the financial goals could be! Adjust these as needed but set retirement goals as soon as you can.

7. Before you invest, check the credibility of the company and professionals you are working with. Go to Investor.gov to find a free, simple, search tool that allows you to find out if your investment

professional is licensed and registered and if they have disciplinary history or customer complaints. *Always* check the background of who is dealing with your money!

> *"Don't save what is left after spending; spend what is left after saving!"*
>
> —Warren Buffett

Retire with Dignity

Investing for retirement doesn't have to be frightening, but it does have to be a part of your financial roadmap. Take it one step at a time. Don't be afraid to ask questions, and don't sign anything that you don't understand. Many times, we get in trouble for the questions we don't ask. A good reference book I recommend is Tony Robbins' *Money Master the Game: Seven Simple Steps to Financial Freedom.* That book is my "financial Bible" when it comes to investing. He speaks in a way that a beginner investor can understand the basics and feel more empowered to make sound investment choices.

Remember, because we worked hard for our income, we should want it to grow. We should desire it to be used for things we believe in and to support our families and futures. Credit card companies know the power of compound interest, and that is why they employ so many tactics to keep you in debt.

You are the stock market *they* are investing in.

You're giving them 25 percent return on their money. They are making a *ton* of money off Americans stuck in debt. It's time to get out of their game and into creating your own winning game with money. Invest properly. Invest with wisdom. Invest for your future.

Section Nine Summary

1. Be cautious of expecting to be fully dependent on Social Security. It's on shaky ground and might not be here when you're ready to retire.

2. To take advantage of the effect of time and compounding interest, get rid of your high interest debt first and then consider investing (even if you're not yet fully debt free).

3. Don't let the vocabulary or foreign concepts stop you from investing. Check out the hacks, ask lots of questions and continue learning.

Section Ten

INVESTING LIFE INTO LIFE

Chapter Thirty-Five

(Final Game)
FINDING YOUR
"OUGHT"

This has been a journey—a journey of making a decision, being truthful with your numbers, knowing you are worthy of your definition of success and dealing with external and internal forces that cause you to spend. Wow! It's been a journey. When you stop and really take stock of just how important it is to understand the financial game being played all around you, it really makes you more aware of both sides of the coin—the offensive and the defensive. There are no professional sports teams that just practice one side of the game. They don't just work on blocking. They don't just focus on shooting. They make sure their teams are creatively strong on *both ends*—the defense and the offense.

I hope by now you understand that it needs to be the same way with your finances.

Once again, the offense consists of the outer game tactics. This is the budgeting, the planning, the goal setting, and managing the net worth numbers. The defense focuses on training areas that aren't so easy to see. This includes your internal beliefs systems, advertising mind tricks, and how marketers can influence your identity to increase your consumption. To be successful in handling your finances, you need to address *both* sides. You need to draw up game plans for both tactics. A weakness on one end could mean disaster.

If you have your goals set and your plans laid out, even if life throws you a life shock, you're better able to absorb it. If one of your best players gets injured, the other teammates are strong enough to compensate for that temporary loss. Your team is strong. With the training you're learning with this book and other resources, you're ready for battle. You've got this!

It's Generosity, Contribution, and Compassion for the Win!

After I figured out this was a game, I then learned how to play it. I learned how to develop my creative skills to create the life I want. Now that I'm winning, I have realized, it's just like Monopoly. You get engrossed in the game, you employ your strategies, and make sure people don't take advantage of you. You invest and have people land on your property and pay you dividends and rent. If you think strategically, you can win the entire tournament! Yet, when the game is over, when all is said and done, the pieces all go back in the box.

Everything you worked hard for goes right back into the box.

This is exactly how life is. All our materials, cars, houses, and out-of-style gadgets go right back into the box, and to someone else, when we pass on.

The only thing that lives on, and escapes this proverbial box, is our generosity, our creative contribution, and our compassion. Think about it. These things, these building blocks of love and purpose, have the ability to outlive the short span of our lives. Consider the most famous examples of this phenomenon, like Maya Angelou, Martin Luther King Jr., Helen Keller, Nelson Mandela, and Anne Frank. These people were not here long, nor were they extremely wealthy, but their contributions will keep making ripples for decades to come.

What are you contributing to that will outlive you?

After I asked myself this thought-provoking question, I knew I wanted to do more than just *win* at this financial game. I desired to create a life of contribution with my life *and my money*. My money needed a mission. My cash needed a cause. My provision needed a purpose. I prayed for God to show me where I was supposed to contribute. How could my creative ideas and my financial resources benefit others around me or even benefit the larger society as a whole? How could I change the world, even if it's just changing a situation in *my world*—my tiny sphere of influence for the better?

After a bit of soul searching, I ended up back at what I excelled at and enjoyed—teaching. My craft is education, and I am a good teacher. That ended up being the foundation of my generosity, contributions, and compassion. "If you just stay in school, you're gonna make it too." The valet's encouraging statement came rushing back to me. "Stay in school, Genein. Stay in what you are gifted in. There is your contribution. There is legacy."

Your Ought: Turning Pain Points to Purpose Points

Sometimes your pain and struggle can be the foundation of where you are called to contribute and have compassion. I have met former drug addicts and prostitutes who now work in those areas to free people from those same afflictions. They know the demons the people are dealing with. They know strategies that helped themselves break free from that lifestyle. They're not afraid to offer a helping hand in those areas.

It was the same for me. My struggle with financial literacy and student loan debt caused me to launch a mentorship program called Alumni360 in 2014. The elementary students I taught were graduating and heading off to middle school and high school. My heart saw them on this conveyor belt heading right into the debilitating financial debt trap my generation got caught in.

Something *ought* to be done. Someone *ought* to do something.

I could no longer sit back and watch this financial suicide happen without doing anything about it. In Alumni360, the graduates of my elementary school come together once a month to learn about financial literacy and creative skills and to tell their stories of purpose to win scholarships.

Since then, many of my students have won scholarships and community opportunities to enhance their academic experiences and professional careers. Several of them have become speakers and leaders in their spheres of influence. To combat the gender pay gap, my female students have taken negotiation workshops to raise their future salaries. All my students have had network training to build their professional network in person and on LinkedIn.

This was a pain point for me. I kept saying, "Someone *ought* to do something about this."

That someone was me.

When you see something and think, *Something* ought *to be done about that*, nine times out of ten, it's God telling *you* to do something about it. It's that creative idea in your spirit. It's that weighing feeling on your heart. It keeps coming back because it's a part of your destiny. It's relentless.

Someone *ought* to do something.

Is that someone you?

Open your eyes, listen to your heart, and your *ought* will find you. Trust me.

> "I'd rather have it said, 'He lived usefully than he died rich.'"
>
> —Benjamin Franklin

It's Your Turn

Jot down an injustice that has caught your attention and keeps coming up into your consciousness. Write down what it is, who it is affecting, and how you can use your resources (finances, time, creativity and wisdom) to help with the problem. Then be clear with your action steps and apply a deadline. Really take the time to reflect on this important part of your destiny.

My Ought
Problem:
First Three Actions I Will Do:
Target Completion Date:

Chapter Thirty-Six
(Final Play)
NEW BEGINNINGS

It is my hope that this book has ignited you to dream something better for your financial life and for your destiny. You are creative and your financial abundance is residing within your creativity. It was my goal for you to learn from my mistakes, experiences, and triumphs to help you create a better destiny for you, your money, and your mission.

You have the opportunity to create the future you desire. Create with passion. Create with wisdom. Create with courage. Hopefully, we can meet someday, and I'll be able to hear how this book played a small role in your success. That would bring a smile to my face and joy to my heart.

Once you realize that it's a creative game and you have the fortitude to play (now knowing the rules), you'll finally believe that you can win. Belief is the movement that opens the door to endless possibilities. No matter what situation you are in now, it can, and will, get better if you just start. Start today.

And I'll be here cheering you on!

God bless.

ACKNOWLEDGMENTS

This book was prompted by God's urging me to be a solution. I thank God for the opportunity to be an amplifier of his voice and be a support for the people. My heart overflows with gratitude as I experience this wild ride, I laughingly call my life. Jeremiah 29:11.

Mom, also known as Gwen Jefferson, you know I always quote the words of Abraham Lincoln when I refer to you. "All that I am and all that I will ever be, I owe to my mother." Even though you didn't give us tons of financial knowledge, you gave us something even more valuable: the ability to be creative, the freedom to be curious, and the tenacity to act, even in the face of fear. Those qualities were priceless, and they have propelled my siblings and me to where we are today. Thank you for your uniqueness and your drive. Thank you for your goofiness and your compassion. Thank you for you. You were and will always be my first teacher. I love you!

To my siblings, Genae Jefferson, Genette Morrison, and Joseph Jefferson. You all are amazing, and I am so grateful that you allowed me to share our journey with the world. Your accomplishments in your fields and society are impressive, and I am constantly in awe of your contributions. Thank you for being a wonderful support and cheerleader of my pursuits. I am honored to not only call you a sister and brother but to also call you friends. Thank you to my little nieces and nephews. I am working hard to change the trajectories for all of us. Thank you, Dad, for giving me a love for reading and seeking wisdom. All is well.

To my coaches and mentors, Coach Tony Magee, Daniel Luna, John Murray, and Pastors Tymme and Aury. Coach Tony, it was a divine appointment that you spoke at my school that clear day in 2014. I needed someone to show me to the next level, and God sent you to me. Thank you for taking me under your wing and giving me the mindset to progress in my personal and professional journey and the confidence to support this evolution. You are a genius.

Daniel, thank you so much for being our first speaker at Alumni360! You have mentored my students, and you are also an inspirational mentor for me. Your wisdom is endless, and your encouragement is breathtaking. You keep me brilliant in the basics.

John Murray, you took this stuttering young lady and turned her into an award-winning speaker. I will never forget the day I walked into your Challengers Toastmasters International club, not knowing what to expect. My spirit knew that this was my club and you were my speech mentor. Thank you for your persistent work with me and helping me master the TEDx stage to share my story. I couldn't have done it without you.

Pastors Tymme and Aury, thank you for being my spiritual mentors throughout these years. You were the first to put me on the platform to teach finances, and I am grateful for your belief in me and the opportunity you bestowed on this girl who had this unusual passion for financial literacy and the creative process. Your encouragement and love have not gone unnoticed, and I am grateful to God for your presence in my life and my family's life.

To those who contributed financially to the publishing of this book, a heartfelt thanks is also sent your way. Your donation is now aligned with this mission of getting people financially fit and creatively courageous. Any wins with this project are now a win for you too. Your partnership means the world to me.

To my major financial contributors: Peter Bloom, my fellow Donorschoose.org board member, I remember how terribly nervous I was at my first board meeting in New York. You made me feel so welcomed with your lightheartedness and humor. Your enthusiasm for our teachers and students is overwhelming. I am so honored to have you as a mentor and to learn under your leadership of such a wonderful organization. Keep creating the magic for our students! Cassie Cox, your love for your students is palpable, and I thank you for your encouraging words throughout the years. Don't lose heart and keep up the great work! Gia Stokes, thanks for your support and your work in the nonprofit sector. You have been a role model for me since I visited you at your home when I was twelve! Angelia Trinidad, thanks for your great entrepreneurship story of how you created the Passion Planner and for supporting me and Alumni360! Keep sharing your story and inspiring many to live their best lives with passion!

David Samuel, I met you on a bus to Mexico during my first mission trip in 1998 and you have been a supportive voice in my life ever since. Thank you for your blunt wisdom and crazy antics to education and entrepreneurship. You keep it real! We will always be friends through these adventures of life! Elizabeth Rodriguez, we have been through so much (and going through stuff right now, too) and it's been an honor watching you grow through life. I'm excited for this next chapter in both of our lives, and I hope we can continue to be a sounding board for one another!

To the De Leon Family, you have become family through your love for my little Shawn. I thank you all for your support of my book, Alumni360 and the GATE parents of NEW Academy Canoga Park. Your mentorship for the NACP/Alumni360 families has not gone unnoticed. God sees your heart, and you all are being strategically set up to win because you work so hard to help others win. I know this to be true. My family adores you all, and Shawn thinks the world of you!

Other amazing contributors to the campaign were Tymme and Aury Reitz, Brenda Contreras, Arturo Vazquez, Corey Heimlich, Ruth Menedez, Matt Ladhoff, Susanne Tedrick, Fannie and Adrian Wright, Tonya and Adrian Moss, Kristy Mersinger, Sherry Sanborn, Rianne Roberts, Reyna Booth, Laura Contreras, Janelle Lin, Cecilia Eriksson, Gina Brady, Tania Mulry, Ruth Mendez, Christian Carreon, Kathleen Hall and Jennifer Graf. Thank you all for supporting me!

Last, but certainly not least, I have to spend some time appreciating the loves of my life, Shayne and Shawn Letford. Shayne, you are not the wind beneath my wings; you are the other wing and we're flying this eagle together! Without you, I certainly couldn't fly as high. I honestly believe

God knew you were my husband before we were even born. "There's this crazy girl who is going to have some crazy *grand* ideas, and her husband needs to be able to handle that." Enter you. Shayne, I hope I support you and your dreams as much as you have supported me. You are an excellent partner in life, and I certainly would not have been able to do a lot of what I am doing without you by my side. With LetfordMedia.com, you created all the websites, logos, and other media for Alumni360 when it was just an idea in my heart. What a blessing you have been to me, my students, and our family. And to my son, Shawn Tyler, Mommy loves you so much. You have such a gift of joy, wisdom and encouragement, even as a baby. I had to feed you early in the morning, like at three a.m., and then retreat to my computer to write this book while you slept. You're such a blessing and we are working hard in order to give you something you can build upon for the next generation. I'll be eagerly awaiting to read your book one day. We love you.

To everyone else, if you have blessed me in any way, please know I send my gratitude to your heart. Thanks to all my family, teachers, mentors, and friends who encouraged me to share my story, write my passion, and speak my truth.

Keep doing work that matters.

Genein Marie

APPENDIX

List of Documents at Creative Wealth Academy.net

Net Worth Sheets

Budget Spending Plans

Goal Sheets

LIST OF
FINANCIAL TERMS

A

APR, annual percentage rate—An annual percentage rate is the annual rate charged for borrowing or earned through an investment. APR is expressed as a percentage that represents the actual yearly cost of funds over the term of a loan

Assets—Something of value that is owned. Appreciating assets, such as stocks, have the potential of increasing in value and/or producing income. Depreciating assets, such as a car, lose value over time. Assets minus liabilities (what is owed) equals net worth.

B

Balance—A balance might be the amount of money present in a checking or a savings account. Balance can also indicate the amount of money remaining to be repaid on a loan.

Bankruptcy—When an individual or a company has insurmountable debt and cannot repay it, it's possible to declare bankruptcy to receive legal protection from the debts. Bankruptcy involves a legal process, possibly including the sale of assets to reduce the debt amount.

Bond—The government or a corporation might issue bonds to investors indicating a specific debt between the business entity and the investor. The government or corporation agrees to pay the investor the face value of the bond and interest for the term of the bond.

Budget—A budget is a written or electronic accounting plan to help manage finances and save money.

C

Charge—Making a charge involves a purchase on a revolving credit account. The consumer borrows the money, which will result in interest charges unless the borrower pays the amount in full before the grace period ends.

Collateral—Some loans require property to assure repayment of the loan. This property is called collateral.

Credit—Credit encompasses money borrowed that a borrower will need to repay.

Credit history—As consumers manage finances, borrowing and repaying money, they develop a credit history that details these transactions. Future loans depend on a solid credit history, because lenders check this information.

D

Debt—A debt is money or goods owed to another individual or to another entity.

Default—A default occurs if a payment is not made according to the terms of an agreement.

Deposit—Placing money into an account is a deposit.

Depreciation—An asset's value might go down over a period of time due to wear and tear, known as depreciation.

Diversify—An investor will typically spread out investment capital among various types of investments, known as diversification. This practice helps reduce investment risks.

E

Earned income—People who work for their wages receive earned income.

F

Finance charge—Lenders charge borrowers finance charges as fees for lending money. Borrowers who pay off a balance within a grace period can avoid finance charges.

Fixed expenses—Some payments do not change from month to month, making them fixed expenses. An example of a fixed expense might be a car payment.

Foreclosure—If a borrower does not make payments on a secured debt, the lender might initiate legal foreclosure proceedings to seize the property associated with the debt. Default on a mortgage could result in foreclosure and auction of the property.

G

Grace period—Revolving credit card lending involves grace periods, wherein borrowers do not have to pay finance charges or interest if they pay balances in full.

I

Income—Money earned from working or earned passively from investments.

Gross income—The total amount of money earned before any taxes, investments, or other deductions are taken out.

Net income—The amount left over after taxes and other deductions have been taken out.

Inflation—A general increase in prices and fall in the purchasing value of money.

Insufficient funds—If an account holder makes a bookkeeping error and writes a check without having at least this much money in a checking account, the bank might return the check due to insufficient funds. Banks often charge penalty fees for insufficient funds.

Interest—Lenders charge a percentage of loan amounts as a fee for the loan, known as interest.

Interest rate—The percentage charged in interest is known as the interest rate.

Invest—People who wish to earn a profit from their money might make purchases or place their money into specific types of accounts, known as investing.

L

Liability—A debt or an obligation that is taking money out of the individual's pocket.

Lien—A lender might place a lien on property in connection with a debt, giving the lender legal right to the property if the borrower defaults on the loan.

Loans—A lender and a borrower can make a legal contract for the borrower to use money given by the lender. The borrower usually pays interest for use of the money and must agree to pay back the money within a specified time.

M

Minimum payment—A loan might specify the smallest payment amount due by the borrower, which would be the minimum payment. Borrowers can pay more than the minimum payment.

Money market account—Investors might deposit money into money market accounts to earn interest on the balance. Investors must maintain a minimum balance.

Mortgage—The loan involved for purchase of real estate is a mortgage.

Mutual fund—A group of investors might hold a collection of different types of assets together. This type of investment provides investors with diversification, which can reduce risks.

O

Overdraw—Attempting to withdraw money from an account, exceeding the account balance, is overdrawing the account.

P

Points—Lenders might add points to the principal amount of a loan. Points are a percentage of the loan amount, due as a lump sum payment.

Principal—The amount borrowed for a loan without interest is the principal. The amount of money invested by an investor is also the principal.

Profit—An investor might make a profit after subtracting the principal invested and any additional amount of money spent in connection with the investment.

R

Return—The amount of money returned to an account holder is typically referred to as the return.

Risk—The risk of an investment is the likelihood that the investor will lose money from the transaction.

S

Secured credit card—A young consumer trying to develop a positive credit history might use a secured credit card. With this type of account, the consumer deposits money to create a balance. The consumer can then make charges up to this balance to demonstrate responsible use of the account.

Securities—Securities might be paper or electronic instruments verifying ownership of stocks or bonds.

Service charges—A financial institution might levy service charges to account holders for the upkeep and maintenance of bank accounts.

Share—Investors who own a piece of a corporation own a share of the company.

Sole proprietor—When one person owns a company, this person is the sole proprietor.

Stock—Companies might issue stock to investors to certify ownership of a part of the company.

T

Taxes—A government typically charges its citizens compulsory fees to help maintain the government.

U

Unearned passive income—When people make money from interest, they are making unearned income.

V

Variable expenses—Some expenses change from month to month, making them variable expenses. Examples of variable expenses include groceries or utility bills.

W

Withdrawal—Removing money from an account is known as withdrawing the money.

LIST OF
INVESTMENT FEES

12b-1 Fee

This charge generally allows fund companies to compensate broker/dealers for selling their funds, with a payment to the representative who sold the fund. This fee is also used to cover the marketing and distribution costs of the investment.

Administrative Fee

Covers recordkeeping and other administrative expenses. It might be charged as a flat account maintenance fee or as a percentage of account value.

Annual Contract Charge

A fee charged by a vendor for administrative expenses.

Commissions (Loads)

A load is a commission the investor pays to purchase (front end) or sell (back end) an investment. Look for no-load investment options to avoid this cost.

Custodial Fee

The charge for safekeeping or physically holding the securities in the account.

Investment Advisory Fee

The fee a fund manager charges to make investment decisions for a mutual fund. Investors don't pay the investment advisory fee directly. Instead, it is deducted directly from the fund's returns. The investment advisory fee is one part of a fund's expense ratio.

Management Fee

Also called the investment advisory fee, this represents the company's cost for managing the money in the fund. (See investment advisory fee.)

Mortality and Expense (M&E) Fee

Mortality fees are paid to ensure that after a death, the beneficiaries will not receive less than what was contributed to the account. These fees typically range from 0.95 percent to 1.80 percent annually. M&E is most often associated with variable annuity accounts.

Surrender Charge (Withdrawal Charge)

This fee is charged as a penalty for withdrawing money (even for transfers) before the required holding period is over. Holding periods can be seven, ten, or even twenty years. The penalty claims a percentage of your account, typically up to 7 percent, but it might be higher.

Wrap Account Fee

Charged by a personal financial advisor, this fee is expressed as a percentage of the client's assets under management. It is in addition to the other fees listed.

BE THE CHANGE: SEED THE CHANGE

Breaking the cycle of poverty and making sure people are financially and creatively educated is now my life's purpose. Making sure you have the education you need to make sound decisions, while still enjoying a creative life, is important to me. I have the honor of writing books, creating programs, and speaking to audiences around the world on these topics that, in my mind, are critical to a life well lived.

My most recent Alumni360 project is the Seed the Change investment initiative program that gets our young people investing earlier in life. We look at people and say, "You should invest!" But then we leave and don't help them get started. So, five years pass, then ten. Then they turn into the millions of other Americans who wait until their late thirties or forties to start investing. This happens because they didn't know *how* to get started. Do you remember how important time is with investments?

With the Seed the Change program, we match professionals, who are investing, with graduating high school employed students. We help them start their first Roth IRA and even "seed" them with $100. This $100 seed communicates, "I believe in you as an investor. I also believe it is so important to start early that I am putting my money where my mouth is. Start now. Be consistent and don't waver!"

The students pledge to continue to invest a minimal amount while getting through school and once they graduate from college and start their careers, they will "seed" another young student just starting out in their adult life. In addition to these professionals "seeding" a young student, they are going to challenge five professional people in their adult circle to "seed" a young person in *their* sphere of influence. It is our hope that the

From Debt to Destiny

ripple effect will never end. Let's get these young people, especially first-generation college students, to become first-generation investors! Be the change you wish to see!

This is how I turned my pain points into points of contribution and generosity. When I started Alumni360, I paid for everything out of my own pocket. The food, the supplies, and the buses for field trips. The most expensive resource I paid was my time. But these kids are worth it—their futures are worth it. Eventually, I found sponsors to come alongside me and build this program.

The Seed the Change program is also growing. I launched it by seeding nineteen-year-old Brenda Contreras, who became a first-generation college student in her family and the first investor. She will then take that $100 I gave her (in honor of my grandmother, Della Cantrell) and pass it on to another young Alumni360 student. Other people are seeding Alumni360 students a well. If you want to join this movement, email me because . . .

This is how we can break the cycle of poverty—with academic *and* financial education. Join us. Visit Alumni360.org/SeedTheChange.

Note to Readers

This publication contains the opinions and ideas of its author. It is intended to provide helpful and informative material on the subjects addressed. The strategies in this book might not be suitable for every individual and are not guaranteed or warranted to produce any particular results.

This book is sold with the understanding that neither the author nor the publisher is engaged in rendering legal, financial, accounting, or other professional advice or service. The reader should consult a competent professional before adopting any of the suggestions in this book or drawing inferences from it.

No warranty is made with respect to the accuracy or completeness of the information or referenced contained herein, and both the author and the publisher specifically disclaim any responsibility for any liability, loss, or risk, personal or otherwise, which is incurred as a consequence, directly or indirectly, with the use and application of any of the contents of this book.

Financial Book List

Money Master the Game: Seven Simple Steps to Financial Freedom —Tony Robbins

The Total Money Makeover: A Proven Plan for Financial Fitness —Dave Ramsey

The Automatic Millionaire: A Powerful One-Step Plan to Live and Finish Rich —David Bach

ABOUT THE AUTHOR

As the 2015 Charter School Teacher of the Year, Genein Letford is a driving force in student equity access and creative and financial literacy. She is the founder of the Creative Wealth Academy, which equips companies and individuals with creative and wealth-building skills. A 2017 TEDx speaker (see https://www.youtube.com/watch?v=XMcxMToduj8), she believes every person deserves the opportunity to develop their talents and contribute positively to the community.

After paying almost $100,000 of debt, Genein realized the importance of early financial literacy, opportunity recognition, and telling your story of purpose. She founded Alumni360, a mentorship organization that equips youth with financial and creative literacy as well as life skills. The Economic Valley Alliance honored her with the Innovation in Education award for her unique approach to entrepreneurship and creativity. In 2019, the Lakers and CoAmerica Bank honored her as a Woman of Philanthropy and she was also awarded with the prestigious BMe Vanguard Fellowship. She speaks around the nation about creative and financial literacy and remains committed to preparing the next generation for a life of success.

In addition to directing Alumni360 and the Creative Wealth Academy, she is a board member of the national nonprofit Donorschoose. org and a financial literacy coach at her local church, Life150. She enjoys writing books on how creativity affects finances and hopes that her books will inspire many people to live their best creative lives. She lives in Los Angeles, California with her creative husband, Shayne and their curious son, Shawn.

Other Books by Genein Letford

Create and Grow Rich Series

- *Create and Grow Rich: For Teachers*
- *Create and Grow Rich: For Organizations*
- *Create and Grow Rich: For Christians*

  Proverbs for Provision: Sixty-Six Proverbs for Creating Wealth with a Purpose

Courses by Genein Letford

Creative Wealth Academy: Creative Health for Financial Wealth

Negotiation 101

Power of Journaling

Proverbs for Provision: Implementing the Proverbs for a Financially Purposeful Life

Visit GeneinLetford.com and CreativeWealthAcademy.Net

Praise for *Creative Wealth Academy*

I've successfully gone through the Creative Wealth Academy with Genein and it was such a blessing to my life. I was able to encounter discipline with my finances and in that workshop you learn so much about yourself and your identity within this whole entire process of putting your creativity and finances together. It's such a successful way to live. You really feel freedom.

—Gerald Castle, actor, dancer

Genein, I wanted to let you know that I paid off ALL of my credit card debt since taking your course. It was something I really wanted to tackle before getting into the other financial areas. It wouldn't have been possible without the key lessons you taught, so I wanted to let you know how much it means to me.

—Alexander Bryant, social media strategist

I had a sit-down meeting with Genein in which we discussed how to manage my finances. She was truly insightful! Genein challenged me to budget and cut some of my costs to save more money every month. I'm thankful for her direct approach and honestly. I'm on a better road to reaching all of my financial goals.

—Shavon Kirksey, actress, entrepreneur

Hearing about happiness, finances and Genein's life story was so inspiring because we don't learn about these things. I never really considered my own net worth until this lecture. Knowing these things early will really help me as I become older. Her speech on happiness and worth really made me feel different. Because of her speech I know I have more of what it takes to become successful.

—Josh Haynes, UCLA student

Thank you Genein, for this financial course. I can't believe how easy you make and explain the steps needed to help me become more successful in my finances. You give such valuable information and implementations needed to make life easier and the financial world more understandable.

—Theresa Dunlap, educator

My husband and I struggled for years with debt. It was crippling to know that so much of our income was taken before we even saw it. Genein personally helped us address the issue. We are now free of all credit card debt and are currently attacking our student loan debt like a beast! Her book taught us tools that helped us see the light at the end of this debt tunnel and we're forever grateful for the hope she brought back to us.

—Genette D. Morrison, M.S, Nurse

Every person needs a push that serves as a reminder of why financial responsibility raises their quality of life. It gives discipline and boundaries. This book helped me plan and dream for the day when the debt noose is eliminated and the world is brighter and lighter. I'll read it every time I need that push!!

—Genae V. Jefferson, M.S, Systems Engineer, DRS Tech

Genein's dedication to spreading financial knowledge to demographics usually not privy to this information is influential and sincere. Generational wealth is the cornerstone for opportunity, and in the absence of it one has to learn from the ground up. This book expertly aides in that goal.

—Joseph Jefferson, M.S, Mission operations engineer, NASA

In the 1980's, I remember being around colleagues who were talking about investments and purchasing Apple stock. I had no idea how to get started or how to buy stocks. After Genein took me to a teacher retirement meeting three years ago, followed later by her financial education class, I was inspired to get my finances in order and get ready for retirement. Unlike some of my co-workers, I feel confident to retire this year, since my debt is paid off and my savings is strong. Working with Genein gave me a light at the end of the tunnel. She is an effective teacher who will help millions reach their creative and financial goals. I'm proud and honored to be her mother.

—Gwen Jefferson, M.Ed, Retired Biology Teacher,
30 years of Service